Be Rich AND Spiritual

Yildiz Sethi

Copyright ©Yildiz Sethi

All rights reserved. No part of this publication may be reproduced, stored in a retrievable system, or transmitted in any form or by any means, electronic, mechanical, photocopy, recording or otherwise, without prior written permission of the copyright owner, except in the case of brief quotations embedded in critical articles or reviews.

Cover design by DESIGNED.co.uk

Third edition

This book is available in kindle book format, details of which are available at Ingram Sparks

ISBN 9780648479123

Dedication

With gratitude to my family, children and grandchildren, and to everyone who has touched my life.

Foreword

Be Rich AND Spiritual is a fantastic book that is in a league of its own when it comes to combining the principles of wealth and spirituality. It goes beyond what we all learned in The Secret by Rhonda Byrne, offering a rare look at what's really running the show that we call 'our life'.

Yildiz took me on a magical journey; explaining the spiritual world concisely and clearly, debunking the myths around karma and other complex spiritual concepts in an easy-to understand way.

She explains how the ancient science of Vedic astrology can help us to create a life with fewer struggles and a greater acceptance of ourselves. This book helps us to understand how we can use Vedic astrology to accurately predict phases of our life which, in turn, allows us to live our lives more productively and meaningfully.

This book had a tendency to call out to me at 1.30 am, so I duly got up several times to drink from its wisdom. I would recommend this book to anyone who is interested in living a spiritually fulfilling life combined with one of material success. And who doesn't want that?

Written by: Tim Wise, Speaker/Trainer/Mentor,

www.timwise.com.au

Special Offers

10% off Yildiz's certified online training

If you love the book then consider taking your practice further.

Simply scan the codes below to receive 10% off Yildiz's:

- Certified Family Constellations online training
- Vedic astrology online

Or go to: https://familyconstellations.com.au/buy-fc-training/

Family Constellations Online training with experiential learning- 12 weeks

10% discount coupon **BRFC10**

Or go to: https://vedicastrology.net.au/buy-your-va-course-now

Vedic astrology online 12 week training

10% discount coupon **BRVA10**

Family Constellations training is certified in Australia and allows the student to obtain insurance and immediately start earning income and helping others.

Please read on to learn more about Yildiz's online training courses.

Family Constellations Online training

Family Constellations is a modality that shows the underlying dynamics, entanglements and generational trauma of individuals in their family systems. Also how these manifest in the present in relationships, parenting, patterns, wellbeing and mental health and their ability to fulfil potential.

This may take place in groups and private sessions, in person or online. The process is brief, experiential, psychodynamic, solution-focused, phenomenological and client-centred. A powerful way to re-order our inner perception of who we are into healthier places. The Constellation process works at the core of who we are as human beings, in a way that is limited or inaccessible with other approaches: Particularly in such a brief intervention.

The process works at several levels of awareness and experience simultaneously. Intellectual, visual, somatic, emotional, energetically and generationally. For Relationships, family, parenting, relational bonding, generational patterns, generational (systemic) trauma and incest. This results in several levels of change taking place simultaneously, as multiple levels of neural pathways realign. Suitable for existing and new practitioners.

The training is fully online with experiential learning component.

Learn Vedic Astrology Online

Learn how to read the magic and mystery of Vedic astrology.

How Yildiz developed the course

After Yildiz was introduced to Vedic astrology she spent years in study, research and practice. She went to courses in India, USA and in Australia and took part in lots of personal study and hundreds of Vedic astrology books. She found some information really useful and applicable and lots of information, confused confusing and not helpful or accurate. She has put in hundreds of hours of study and practice to find out what works accurately.

This is what she offers you this this course.

An honest open and practical approach to Vedic astrology in looking at the soul's journey.

Learning Vedic Astrology

You will learn by listening. There is an audio for each lesson.

You will learn by reading. There are course notes and charts for each lesson.

You will learn by doing. There are exercises at the back of 11 lessons for you to test yourself.

You may check your answers with the answers section included.

You may repeat each lesson several times.

You will listen and work through the course notes at your own pace.

Do it as fast or as slow as you want – It's up to you.

The course is designed to build your knowledge as you go through it.

You will be shown how to develop your skills in practical applications as you are shown how to navigate through chart information and build up an analysis.

All that's left after this is, Practice, Practice, Practice and ENJOY

Table of Contents

INTRODUCTION 1

ABOUT THE AUTHOR 3

Chapter 1 - A Rich Life 5

Chapter 2 - The Law of Attraction 12

Chapter 3 - The Illusion 21

Chapter 4 - Consciousness 27

Chapter 5 - Our Dilemma: Expansion of the Natural Order 36

Chapter 6 - A Metaphor for Life: Fullness 48

Chapter 7 - Acceptance 52

Chapter 8 - Wealth Readiness, Life Purpose 58

Chapter 9 - The Cosmic Map 75

Chapter 10 - Richness of the Spirit 81

Chapter 11 - Creation, Destiny and Free Will 91

Chapter 12 - Taking Control 98

Chapter 13 - Worthiness 109

Chapter 14 - Being in the World 117

Chapter 15 - Gratitude and Abundance 128

Chapter 16 - Change 135

Chapter 17 - Family Constellations: Systemic Solutions for Success 141

Chapter 18 - Greatness 150

Chapter 19 - Steps to Becoming Rich AND Spiritual 159

Chapter 20 - Enjoy the Journey 176

RESOURCES 179

INTRODUCTION

In my work with people over many years, I have been struck by the growing levels of frustration, disappointment and confusion over their engagement with the ideas espoused by the movement surrounding the Law of Attraction and The Secret.

The purpose of writing this book is to give a fuller perspective of our creative potential and how to utilise it in being BOTH Rich AND Spiritual. I have used much of my knowledge and experience with clients and from my own life to put this book together for those who are ready to live more freely and abundantly.

I am a counsellor, clinical hypnotherapist, family constellations and personal development facilitator and trainer, Vedic astrologer, ex-physics and chemistry teacher, mother and grandmother. In a nutshell, I have a passion for assisting people to free their minds so that they can live more fully in the world. In this book, I explain the problems that we encounter in our endeavour to fulfill our potential and also provide many possible solutions towards transformation.

At this time of our development as human beings, I feel that it is appropriate to incorporate the proven wisdoms and spiritual knowledge of the past with the latest innovations in personal development and an understanding of the functioning of the mind. In this way, we are able to arrive at a deeper understanding of our human potential. Of course, when looking at our potential, spirituality must also be considered, because we are beings with a consciousness and a soul that is very much on a path and journey. Throughout this text, the spiritual journey is given a broad view from which you may draw on to formulate your own developing spiritual philosophy and perspective.

I put forward a revolutionary and unique perspective of how our realities are created. In order to do this subject justice, there is an extensive exploration

INTRODUCTION

of what holds us back from stepping into our greatness. Such a text would be incomplete without sharing the ways to resolve such blocks by following clearly set out steps for material and spiritual growth.

Through a deeper understanding of the workings of the mind, the reader can gain a deeper knowledge of their inner power. Within this, aspects of the conscious and unconscious mind are discussed, to show how blocks to success may form and how these can sabotage many well-formed goals. In exploring the blocks, I present valuable knowledge of how they may be resolved or reformed towards healthier, happier and more successful outcomes.

As a Vedic astrologer, I have incorporated elements of my knowledge that are pertinent to becoming rich and spiritual and, in particular, I provide a fuller understanding of karma and its impact on wealth creation. I dispel myths and misunderstandings about karma and the role it plays in our lives as our greatest spiritual teacher. Unfortunately, karma is often seen by many people in the West as punishment, or as providing very little freedom in how and what we create, or how we respond. Many people think that it takes away freedom, which I show throughout this book to be very much not the case. Knowledge of karma is invaluable in raising awareness, especially when we understand that it is synonymous with elements of the mind and free will.

Throughout this book, several ways of transforming or resolving unwanted patterns of thinking and feelings are provided. Transformation is possible and often occurs naturally for many of us, which demonstrates that we are indeed free to create our own realities in any way we choose.

As a facilitator of family constellations, I introduce this powerful, brief, experiential, solution-focussed, psychotherapeutic methodology as a leading-edge way to resolve self-sabotage and, hence, allows each of us to pursue our full potential. Throughout this self-help, personal development book, there are clear guidelines that can be followed to become rich and spiritual, if you choose.

ABOUT THE AUTHOR

Yildiz Sethi is an Australian woman of Turkish Cypriot and English origins, born in England and living in Brisbane, Australia. She started her career as a physics and chemistry teacher, which she enjoyed for many years before transitioning to Vedic astrology at a sensitive time in her life. This led to a fascination with the psychological patterns that hold people back and to an exploration to find the most effective ways to facilitate change in herself and others. She did further studies to become a counsellor, clinical hypnotherapist and family constellations' facilitator and trainer.

ABOUT THE AUTHOR

Yildiz is now deeply involved in personal development, including Vedic astrology teaching, Family Constellation seminars and training, and she runs a private practice in Brisbane, Australia. She is passionate about helping people free their minds so as to make the most of their lives.

Having come from a working-class background herself, she has expanded her own horizons significantly in all spheres - psychologically, emotionally, practically, spiritually and financially, to create her present reality. By exploring and developing her ability to create and manifest her reality in a tangible way, she has a wealth of unique knowledge and practical experience from her own life journey and from the facilitation of others,' that she shares with you, in your quest to becoming rich and spiritual.

Qualifications

Master of Applied Social Science (counselling),
Graduate Diploma in Counselling, Diploma in Clinical Hypnotherapy, Bachelor of Education, NLP Practitioner, Ego State Therapy Practitioner.

Vocations

Family Constellations facilitator and trainer.
Vedic astrologer and teacher.

Contact

https://yildizsethi.com
https://rapidcorehealing.com
https://familyconstellations.com.au
www.vedicastrology.net.au

Chapter 1

A Rich Life

You have chosen to read this book either because you are curious about the topic or you really want to know how you can be materially rich and also have spiritual richness. Being rich and spiritual may appear to be polar opposites for many people, but I am proposing that this does not need to be the case. How would it be if these could work together? Perhaps being rich and spiritual, is what we are here for.

The purpose of this book is to address the confusion and conflicts that many people experience when they consider wealth and spirituality. There has been much said separately about each one, but not so much about these together. Even though hints or assumptions of spirituality are intimated or assumed in both the Law of Attraction and *The Secret*, they are not addressed directly, or in any great depth. It's my wish, through this book you come to understand your individual relationship with money and spirituality and find more comfort with these aspects of life, in ways that allow you more freedom. My wish is that you find a way to be wealthy and maintain your integrity in being spiritual.

There are many books about creating wealth, so why have I written another? Because vital areas of knowledge have been omitted and assumptions made, that make this area illusive and fraught with frustration and obstacles. Many of you reading this book may already have been consciously focussing on manifesting more wealth into your life and have followed the theory and guidelines of the Law of Attraction with some, to little success, and are wondering why it's not working for you. Some of you may have just started to explore these possibilities and require more understanding. As you have chosen this book, it's likely that you are ready to know how it is possible to be rich and maintain or deepen your spiritual experience, and for these aspects of life to be comfortable bedfellows – with you not having to make a choice of either wealth, or spirituality. This indicates that you have a conscious wish to enjoy financial affluence without guilt.

I invite you to have a pen and paper at hand to jot down ideas as they come to you that may be useful, and to take the time to reflect on the exercises where they appear in the book.

Here is a little about myself. I started life as the eldest of seven children in the very working-class, industrial heartland of England in a multicultural famil,y in a council estate. My father was Turkish Cypriot immigrant with some African roots and my late mother was English. Being born into this family, culture and socio-economic group in England had many gifts, but also major challenges. I found I was faced with a range of choices. The silent expectation from my family and society was that I stay in my place and do my duty as a good working-class girl. While on another level, I was aware of having access to education that made it possible to expand my horizons to include other possibilities. I could, as many people do, have stayed in this place psychologically, economically, educationally, socially and geographically or aspire to something else.

At this point, I need to make it clear that I have a deep respect for those of my family and friends who had different life paths to me and made different choices, and stayed. As I believe we all need to follow our hearts if we are to be true to ourselves. I followed my heart and chose my path.

As a child, I was aware of wanting several things, such as good relationships and a more affluent lifestyle, including travel. I aspired to be a science teacher, or a psychologist and an author.

Even as a young child, I knew I had a choice, even though it was a hard one, because change is not for the faint-hearted. Aspiring to move through social, economic, cultural, educational and philosophical barriers is not an easy path to commit to. This was my choice, but I also believe that I was aware of my life purpose or path too. I was curious to see what I could create in my life from that point onwards. Fortunately for me, there were no real expectations of me, other than those I have already mentioned and those that I imposed on myself.

I am very aware that to be born in England, in itself, was a great blessing, as education and medical care was freely available. Furthermore, the reformation and development in the United Kingdom during the second half of the last century with the embracement of multiculturalism, gender equality, social and economic reform, while somehow paradoxically maintaining social class, to a large extent, produced a dynamic social structure. This made the United Kingdom a complex, contrary melting-pot from which to grow, in a way that was not possible in many other counties of the world. So I do consider myself fortunate in many ways. However, change requires vision, effort and persistence for most of us and later in this book, I explore the possible reasons for this.

Through a long list of choices and also destiny (not my choice), I did not go to university and had to leave school at the age of sixteen. I chose to become a medical laboratory technician, by seeking a job that I found interesting and that would provide further formal education, as I had a hunger for knowledge. I loved science and wanted to study more and knew this career would provide me with this opportunity. It turned out to be invaluable in my later life. I married young, had two children and eventually went to university to become a physics, chemistry and multicultural religion teacher in my early thirties. Thereby starting my high school teaching career. By this time, we had moved to a market town in England, bought a house and my husband was doing very well in his career, so life had significantly changed.

We migrated to Australia where I continued teaching for many more years until a fateful time on holiday in Byron Bay, where I met two Vedic astrologers in one week. Even though up to that point, I had no idea what Vedic astrology was. This was an introduction to a new way of looking at life and spirituality that I found mind-blowing. So much so, that I became deeply engrossed in its study and, within a relatively short time, I left high school teaching to become a Vedic astrologer, much to my own and others surprise. Interestingly, I had loved teaching so much up to that point, that I had expected to stay until retirement.

This was a risky and life-changing career shift, that was not supported by anyone else at that time. I was probably perceived by others to be having a meltdown of some sort. Indeed, my last year of teaching was tough, because I was experiencing an inner turmoil of wanting to become an astrologer full time, while another part of me was arguing that this was a crazy plan, as I was a good teacher and had worked hard to build a very good body of knowledge and practice and was good with students. In addition, I was worried about what others would think of me in making such a radical change. This conflict carried on until I became physically ill and had to take time off with severe digestive problems, that tests suggested were pre-cancerous.

This was enough to help me finally make a choice and I left to embark on becoming an astrologer.

This was difficult financially, as I went from a moderate, steady salary to little, or nothing. However, my husband was still doing well in his career and our children were at university, so things were fine. In the meantime, I lost my identity, to which I found I had a great attachment, as I started again in my middle years to redefine myself. Fortunately, with good alternative medical help, my health recovered over the following year or so.

I learned Vedic astrology very quickly, as it felt so familiar to me. Almost like putting an old, comfortable item of clothing on. However, upon seeing Vedic astrology clients for readings, I became aware, that many of them had deeply rooted problems and I was really aware that I needed to tread carefully. Even though I wanted to help, I had a strong wish to do no harm and became increasingly aware of my limited knowledge in terms of the mind and emotions.

On another level, I was also becoming more and more intrigued with karmic patterns, including my own, and really felt a need to find out what could be done to change them, at a deep, unconscious and karmic level. This led me to the study of counselling and, having done that, I was happy with the results for a while.

However, it didn't take too long to realise, that I was still searching for something deeper, to be able to make significant changes with the people seeking my help in a shorter time span. I didn't see the point of long term therapeutic processes. Hence, I became a clinical hypnotherapist and neuro-linguistic programming (NLP) practitioner, which I was happier with as these allowed me to help my clients in a deeper and faster way.

Then one day, while I was browsing in a book shop, a particular book seemingly shone out at me from the shelf. It was a small, brown, apparently inconsequential book called *Acknowledging What Is* by Bert Hellinger (1999). I bought it and was totally inspired by its contents. This was my introduction to the practice of family constellations, and so I moved on I remember making a silent wish to be able to witness it in person one day. I then let go of the idea, because Bert Hellinger, the founder, was in Germany and at that time, I was in Sydney, Australia, so it didn't seem possible that I would be able to meet him. However, a couple of years later, while travelling through India with my then husband, we were at an Ashram in Pune and, while walking through it, I was faced with a banner saying, 'Family Constellations Demonstration'. Of course, we went in and was again inspired. We cancelled the rest of our holiday, stayed to do a workshop and then took part in facilitator training with Svagito Liebermeister, the author of *The Roots of Love* (2006). Later that same year, I continued training in Spain with Svagito and was thereby happily initiated into the magical and deeply powerful process of family constellations.

Family Constellations is a means by which systemic and generational issues may be explored and resolved in an experiential process. I believe such generational issues are also karmic in coming through past lives. As the constellation theory and practice is a highly effective process, to assist with generational issues that may be felt in the present. This largely overtook my therapeutic practice in becoming a central part of my work with clients for several years, in seminars and my private practice. I consider myself very fortunate to have found family constellations in such a fortuitous manner.

It has been fourteen years since I left school teaching and, since then, my life has expanded significantly in many directions; financially, emotionally, spiritually and geographically (I am now in Brisbane), and it continues to expand. Since my major career change from school teaching, I have done extensive higher learning of all kinds and also travelled a lot. As well as studies in counselling and hypnotherapy, I have learned astrology in Sydney, India and Switzerland, and had family constellations' training with Bert Hellinger himself in Austria, and with many other internationally-acclaimed trainers in Spain, Germany, India and Australia. I am now an author of three books, *Stardust on the Spiritual Path* (2014), *Rapid Core Healing* (2016) and this one, *Be Rich AND Spiritual (2014)*.

It has been a big journey that has not always been easy, but it has been very worthwhile. There were many times when it was tough and I could have given up, but somehow I maintained my visions, while getting on with daily living, step by step.

Perhaps I have also missed out on opportunities. Who knows how many times I have given up, not maintained my vision, not taken advantage of potential opportunities or missed choices that could have been more advantageous? I will never know and I have found its wise not to dwell on this. Nevertheless, I have become richer, more spiritual, am still in the process of growth in both of these aspects of living and am very much enjoying the journey.

The purpose of telling you a little about my life is to let you know that I might be much like many of you, as I was not born with a silver spoon in my mouth, though I do know that I have also been very fortunate.

CHAPTER 2

The Law of Attraction

It is my view that the Law of Attraction leaves many unanswered questions, so let's look at its basic ideas.

It makes use of positive psychology and the idea that we create our own reality from our thoughts. Simply put, it implies that, by being clear and passionate about our thoughts and desires, we can create what we want in our lives.

The steps in the Law of Attraction go something like this:

- Relax and meditate for 5-10 minutes.
- Have a clear intention.
- Make your request to the universe in words, pictures or both, with gratitude, as if it is already a reality.
- Put some emotion into your vision or thoughts and feel how good it is to have received your wish.
- Show gratitude for all the things you have in your life.
- Have faith and trust that whatever you truly desire, will come true in an instant.

The ideas involved in the Law of Attraction can be traced back through time to some of the earliest wise and successful people of the world, regarding their understanding of themselves and humankind as creators.

> "A man is made by his beliefs. As he believes, so he is."
> Bhagavad-Gita from Ancient India.

In more recent times, Wallace D. Wattles in *The Science of Getting Rich* (2007), first published in 1910 was a pioneer in this area. He gave a very potent message about the power of the mind to create reality. Many ideas from his book have been used in *The Secret* by Rhonda Byrne (2006) and the Law of Attraction writings and teachings. It seems that this knowledge goes back into our distant past to the wise, great men and women of humanity. Wallace refers to the Vedas as one of the sources of his knowledge that he examined while looking at the laws of creation. The Vedas are a vast body of ancient Indian knowledge, dating back to 5,000 BC.

> *"The theory that One is All, and All is One: That one substance manifests itself as the seeming many elements of the material world, is of Hindu origin, and has gradually been winning its way into the Western world for two hundred years."* Wallace Wattles (2007)

The Secret and the movement that came out of that, the Law of Attraction, has promoted some of the principles of this philosophy, but has left out many of the conditions by which it may be understood and used more effectively. *The Secret* shows speakers sharing the benefits of the Law of Attraction in their lives and encouraging others to do the same. There is even an unspoken suggestion that such a manifestation can be easy. This message has been encapsulated by many personal development groups and is being fed to mass audiences all around the world, even as I write. This is a Law of Attraction philosophy that underpins the inspiration and thrust of the personal development movement that says: think, visualise and act positively to create a different reality.

While I agree overall with this message, it is over-simplified because there is much left out. The purpose of writing this book is to fill you in on some of the major elements and foundations that have not been explained or understood by the Law of Attraction movement.

Unfortunately, many people are being persuaded to spend large amounts of money to be initiated into this overall foggy and incomplete knowledge. Many people are lured into personal development seminars, where they do indeed come away feeling motivated, because their adrenalin is surging with new ideas of possibilities. However, they are not shown the deeper secrets beyond engaging in positive thinking that are being used by those running the expensive seminars; Who are indeed becoming rich. For most people, once they go back to their own realities, their motivation wanes as the hum drum of practical, everyday life takes over, during the following days and weeks. This is because no real change has taken place in the deeper recesses of their minds.

If you have attended such seminars and have received deep and significant changes that did change your life, that is great! But, for most people, this is not the case. Many people are now poorer because they have spent significant amounts of money that has not helped them make the changes they need to make, in order to become rich. There are many people who are disappointed and disenchanted with what they have done so far in using this theory. Because what has been presented has not helped them to make the deeper changes necessary to enable them to create a more abundant and satisfying life.

I am possibly going against the flow of what is being accepted by the personal development fields by discussing its shortfalls and by later revealing the conditions that are necessary for using the Law of Attraction more successfully, but this is the purpose of my book.

There is no doubt that being positive will change your life in many respects. I know this because it has changed mine significantly. There was a time when I ran a set of negative scripts in my mind about being tired, not so healthy, not good enough, not having enough money and being powerless to change my life. Changing these scripts did indeed change my life. It changed my health, energy levels and my sense of empowerment, worthiness and wealth. These are significant changes that can form a good basis for attracting more good things, including wealth, into your life. However, it takes time, because it is a gradual refining process of thoughts and the development of a willingness to be persistent and vigilant in this task. That's what makes the difference. Often, it seemed like slow progress and it was only when looking back to where I was before, that I could see the significant changes in my inner world and hence my life.

Deepak Chopra in *Quantum Healing* (1990) made the point that there is a connection between the mind and the body. He noticed that thoughts affect the body via the brain's neural pathways. It has been found that thoughts are energetic vibrations that travel along the neural pathways to each body cell. All thoughts, both positive and negative, go through this mind/body pathway. Positive thoughts have a positive effect and negative thoughts have a negative effect. Both impact the mind and body cells. Hence, the organs and body systems as well. This means that feeding the direct link between your mind and body with positive thoughts gives a totally different, outcome compared to negative thoughts. Positive thoughts and feelings enhance vibrational energy to body tissues, and negative ones do the opposite. So, changing what you think or say to yourself, does have an effect on your mind and body. It has to. Changing negative self-talk messages or expectations to positive ones can only increase your wellbeing and, hence, change your life experience. Louise Hay (1999) presented a similar message in *You Can Heal Your Life*. The core themes of these messages have been at the centre of much transformational and personal development thinking into the present and they are very much at the centre of the Law of Attraction and *The Secret*. Such thinking is also the basis of positive psychology, neuro-linguistic programming (NLP), coaching and personal development.

Of course, living with a positive frame of mind has to be beneficial. I like to live with positive thoughts, actions and feelings wherever possible and I do believe that this makes a huge difference to the art of living well. In addition, having an understanding about how, what we put out into the world influences what comes back to us and that what we create, is vital and an essential next step in realising that we are creators. I will explain more about this later.

For now, you can start to make those inner changes and notice the difference over the next day, week, month or year. With commitment and persistence, you should notice real differences in a month or so. Initially, you may be dismayed by the amount of negative self-talk you find is present in your mind. What you are giving yourself on a minute-by minute or day-by-day basis. Don't let this awareness discourage you as this is a learning about what you have been doing to yourself, so that you can take it on board and change it. You can start to change your thoughts and actions in progressively better ways. Awareness is important as a vital step prior to a decision to change. If you continue to pull yourself up and consciously change problematic self-talk, they will begin to recede as your positivity grows.

Before you begin, it is useful to notice what your self-talk is now. Jot down what you say to yourself automatically over the next few days. Notice the quality of your thoughts. Are they happy and optimistic, or are they critical, angry or complaining, etc? Whatever they are, they are being felt by each body cell, because your brain is linked to each cell through neural pathways. If you understand this, you can have an appreciation of the potential power you have to change your life in many respects, because much of it comes from your mind.

The main 'proof' or 'evidence' that advocates of the Law of Attraction and *The Secret* present to us, are frequently long lists of inspirational people, such as Einstein or Bob Proctor, to name a couple, of whom the use of *The Secret* is said to be 'the secret' of their success. While there is no doubt that such people were inspirational, creative and have the ability to manifest and teach us all a great deal, it can be problematic to put their success down to a simple list of steps to follow like a 'recipe for success.' This is far too simple and potentially misleading and has and is causing a lot of disappointment and suffering. As I have already said, while I am in favour of positive psychology, I am also cautious of over-simplistic solutions implying success for everyone, without clear instructions of the conditions that need to be understood and addressed first.

This may appear, at face value, to be easy but, if it was, there would be no need for this book.

I am constantly coming across people who are struggling financially and are frustrated with the poor results they are achieving through visioning, affirmations, motivational and personal development of all kinds. They have either given up and feel angry or let down by the promise of the wealth creation movement, or really want to know what is really going on and how to work with it, in a more productive way. Many people say that they cant control their mind. They forget or have never known, that they are in charge and if they've let their mind be ruled by fears and anxieties, it will continue unless we stop it. It's up to each of us to take charge of our own minds' if we are to take charge of our reality and what we create.

While I agree with the main ideas behind the Law of Attraction, the steps are not so clear for most of us. Simple though they are, they are not necessarily easy to follow. They require levels of understanding, personal development and, finally, for many people, absolute unwavering focus, faith and some practical structure, to achieve positive change. In order to understand how creation works, there are several points we need to consider, the first of which is the need to become clearer about your life purpose.

I was a psychotherapist in Sydney in about 2005 when a client, who I will call Mary, came for her session, looking very happy and excited. I found this unusual because she had been quite sad during the few previous sessions we'd had. She was seeking help in her struggle to put her life back together after her divorce. She was struggling with losing her home, her identity as part of a couple and her need to become financially independent. In the conversation that followed, she told me that she was getting ready to move to a new house. Although Mary had been renting, she said that she was moving to her new home soon, a grand ocean-view house in Sydney. Upon asking what had happened to turn her finances around, she told me that she was watching the DVD, *The Secret,* every morning and night. She was visualising herself living in this splendid house that was going to be auctioned soon. When I asked how she intended to pay for it, she said she was going to buy a winning lottery ticket that would allow her to buy the house. Mary said that she could see herself winning the lottery. She was very excited and animated as she said that she could see herself living there and was so looking forward to moving in.

As a counsellor, this was a dilemma for me. In my mind, I briefly thought about challenging her dream and talking to her about the low probability of her lottery ticket being the winner, to try to reduce the likelihood of disappointment she didn't win. However, I also thought of all the people in the world who did win such lotteries. Someone had to win. Perhaps putting doubt in her mind when she appeared to have none may have been damaging to her ability to manifest her dream. Perhaps, slim as her chance appeared to me, she could win her house. As this was not causing any harm to anyone, I decided to leave Mary with her dream and her secret and we proceeded to work on other areas of her life for that session. We made another appointment for a date after the auction. Mary arrived on that day looking very flat and depressed. The dream was gone, because she didn't have the winning lottery ticket. Now we could look at it and explore what she really wanted in her life. It turned out that money or a big house was not really what she most wanted. She wanted security and financial stability, so that she could pursue her artwork without the stress of financial pressure. She also wanted to resolve her feelings over her ex-husband and find a more appropriate relationship. We began to work on how she could achieve her desire for financial security, so that she could find time for her artistic pursuits. Mary did move on into her new life later with some optimism and wisdom from this situation.

Even though Mary had felt sure that she knew what she wanted, she hadn't. She wasn't clear. Sydney is a decadent city, with wonderful landscapes, where real estate and stunning ocean views are status symbols and desired by many. It appeared to her that successful, happy people live in such homes. Mary had really wanted the happiness of successful relationships most of all and freedom from financial worries. The ocean-view house was a symbol, probably the result of the conditioning of living in a glossy, materialistic society, where it is believed that money brings happiness and is the primary measure of success. There was a lot more going on below the surface than Mary's apparent wish or desire for the house.

I invite you to become clearer about your desire to become rich by completing the following exercise.

What is your goal? If you don't have, one create one now. You may change or fine tune it at any time.

- Notice your involuntary thoughts.
- Repeatedly change them into more positive ones
- What benefits would being rich give you?
- What excites you?
- What makes you happy?
- What are your natural talents or interests?
- What would you change in your life if you were rich?

Here I will share the seven steps to becoming rich and spiritual that will be explored throughout this book.

1. Worthiness
Your level of worthiness is the major indicator of what you attract into your life.

2. Imagination
You must be able to imagine other possibilities in order to create them.

3. Intention
A clearly defined intention helps to maintain a focus to steer your life.

4. Motivation
Motivation is a measure of how much you want what you are aiming for and how much energy you are prepared to put into it.

5. Courage
Courage is required to expand your horizons and define yourself.

6. Action
Action will drive your intention. Without action, your intention will remain a dream.

7. Gratitude
Genuine gratitude for what you have and what you are creating, will ensure that abundance continues to flow.

Consider your goal and go through each step to rate it on a 0-10 scale. Notice if this changes as you go through this book. This will be a very good indication of where you may need to focus your development and growth to make sure your inner world is ready to be rich and spiritual.

It's simple, but not so easy

CHAPTER 3

The Illusion

There are myths about living that many of us are conditioned to believe in. This may be through family, society, nursery rhymes and cultural mythology or ancient archetypes of human consciousness. While much of this starts in childhood, it often lingers on into adulthood unless we examine them and make appropriate changes.

They go something like this:

1. Prince or Princess Perspective

There is a God-like figure looking out for you and guiding you to make sure you have a happy and enjoyable life. He/she is always there to save you from making mistakes and having to suffer. You are really a prince or princess and it is only natural and right that you are born into a perfect loving family who understand you and give you exactly what you want and need. From such a wonderful childhood, you naturally grow into a balanced and confident adult.

Further, in reaching adulthood, you find your soul mate easily and this is a person that fits you perfectly. You have so much in common that you live together in harmony and love and are able to produce your own perfect family. You and your partner have good careers and easily accrue wealth so that you can enjoy the lifestyle you desire.

Everyone recognises and agrees that this is what you deserve. There is only love, comfort and harmony in your life and your purpose is to be happy and enjoy your life.

Somehow, we frequently start life, believing we are special and destined for a charmed life in all respects. This is what many of us wish and hope for and often deeply believe in childhood, adolescence and into adulthood. In fact, many of us so deeply believe it, that we go through life affronted by how 'wrong' life or the world is, by not fitting into our version of how it 'should be'. Many of us still hold remnants of this myth in our mass consciousness and at our core. We are often deeply distressed when this is not realised and start to face reality.

Many of us discover that:

- God does not save us from our poor choices and the resultant suffering.
- our family does not really understand us, or know how to give us what we need;
- we are not so balanced;
- we are confused about ourselves and our place in the world;
- finding a soul mate can be a life-long search, with some being lucky and others being disappointed;
- once in relationship, its often not so simple because it is frequently both pleasurable and also challenging;
- becoming wealthy is often not so simple or easy to achieve or maintain; or

There appears to be a sharp distinction between how we would like life to be and how it is for many of us. So, what can we realistically expect? What is living really about?

Here we have the beginnings of an understanding of some of the deep undercurrents in mass thinking that largely operate subconsciously and are supported and promoted by fiction and the media. When the process of living gradually reveals much of these beliefs to be illusions, we are challenged to find new meaning, or a new story of ourselves, or alternatively, we may choose to rage at the unfairness of the world.

2. Yogic Perspective

Here is another story from the Eastern traditions. The yogic perspective coming from the yogic tradition of ancient Indian philosophy explains that we all come from the creative energy of omnipresence. We come into the physical world and enter onto the wheel of life and death on the reincarnation cycle. By dropping into the physical realm, we lose consciousness of our spiritual source, as we grapple with the reality of survival, and learn to master our physicality as we go through many lives towards self-discovery. The journey of life involves experiencing ourselves in many ways, primarily through relationships and in our attempts to fulfil our desires. Generating wealth is one important part of this experience. All of these experiences lead to a gradual coming out of the illusions we have of ourselves, others and our existence, as we let go of false beliefs and learn to master ourselves, our minds and emotions. When we're ready, we can awaken to ourselves as spiritual beings in a physical plane.

From this perspective, we return to 'all that is' at death, between lives, to assess each experience before being drawn back into life for more experiences. Over aeons of time, we embark on the process of refining ourselves until we have discovered all there is to know about ourselves in this realm. This is the journey towards enlightenment that results in eventually breaking free of the cycle of life and death to become part of omnipresence.

A very simple interpretation of this is that we come into life from a purely spiritual existence to discover who we really are by experiencing ourselves in a physical world. By discovering who we are, we also need to discover 'how' we are when faced with all manner of situations.

This involves how we cope with situations involving:

- physical survival;
- dealing with our own and others emotional needs;

- our thoughts and desires;
- how easily or otherwise we cooperate with others;
- how we deal with our impulses;
- how we deal with our successes and failures.

Through all of these experiences, we come to know and understand ourselves. Relationships with others are vital. Our interactions with others provide us with a mirror of our actions and affects on others. How are we received and what effects or impacts do we have on others. Once we can start to assimilate this information, we can begin to refine and develop ourselves. Find more harmony in our inner world and with fellow human beings.

In this broad tradition, it is largely accepted that such a quest is far too large for one life alone. One life is too short to provide the necessary experiences to complete this extensive exploration of refining thoughts, feelings and behaviours on the journey towards discovering ourselves as spiritual beings. Only through many lives, and being born into many different stations in life, both male and female, through countless possible scenarios, can we possibly come to see who we are. Through many lives, we gradually refine our thoughts and actions towards discovering and revealing our true selves. This is the jewel.

3. A Modern View

As a counsellor, hypnotherapist, family constellations' facilitator and Vedic astrologer, my knowledge and experience with many clients has led me to the belief that perhaps both views 1 and 2 (and others) may be true, in that we are multi-dimensional beings, and this, in turn, may form 'a modern view'.

In 'a modern view', perhaps the story goes something like this. We separate from the oneness of universal energy to experience ourselves in a different way. Discover how we are when we seemingly separated from universal energy into a new life and find ourselves perhaps on our own in a purely material plane. We start off as pure and innocent and ignorant of who we are. Gradually, through many experiences and many lives, we begin to discover ourselves. We experiment in each life and frequently within one life, with a range of beliefs and expectations in order to find out what makes us happy. Because, ultimately, we are always looking for what we've lost in being separated from the Oneness of All That Is. The connection to love and happiness that we know we once had. Hence, we look for love through relationships, fulfilling our goals, creating wealth and fulfilling our desires.

Of course, there are many other important, and probably equally valid, mythology stories from all religions, cultures and aboriginal dreaming, from all corners of the world, that have common themes and deep spiritual significance.

How you view yourself in the world is an important reflection of how you experience your life. If you still have beliefs pertaining to being a prince or princess, as mentioned in myth one, you may experience the world as unfair, unjust and harsh. You may still be waiting for life to come and pick you up and take you into a perfect story.

If you have a view of yourself in the yogic tradition, you will have an idea of yourself as part of the flow of life, connected both to the practical and spiritual elements of life with lots of time to work it all out, through many lives.

If you have a view of yourself from the modern view, you will know that all experiences are of value, unconditionally. They are all part of the journey through the awakening process and exist to be lived and enjoyed, because the journey itself is of greatest value.

Yes, we are here to be happy and to find joy, but we have to find or create it.

The Illusion

What is your myth or world view of life?

What impact does it have on the way you view yourself and those around you?

Reality is in the eye of the beholder.

Chapter 4

Consciousness

As human beings, we are constantly in the process of making meaning of everything in our experience, and this is unique to each of us. We are totally free to make whatever meaning we want of everything. Without limitation. This is our freedom. Our experience becomes our meaning and, hence, our reality. We are conscious beings, although an understanding of consciousness is something that remains elusive, as is shown in the following quote:

> *Further, recognition of the unique properties of consciousness was given by Nobel Laureate in physics, Niels Bohr, who remarked, "We can admittedly find nothing in physics or chemistry that has even a remote bearing on consciousness. Yet all of us know there is such a thing as consciousness, simply because we have it ourselves. Hence, consciousness must be part of nature, or, more generally, of reality, which means that quite apart from the laws of physics and chemistry, as laid down in quantum theory, we must also consider laws of a different kind." Such laws might well include the law of reincarnation, which govern the passage of consciousness from one physical body into another. Coming Back AC.* Bhaktivedanta Swami Prabhupada, p xv (1995).

In summary, Niels Bohr makes the point that there is a need to find new ways to consider the nature of consciousness because the scientific methodologies we have so far, are not equipped to explore this level of human experience.

Our minds are powerful. Our minds that are made up of both conscious and unconscious elements simultaneously, with the conscious part of the mind making up a maximum of only 7% for even the most aware and developed of us. The conscious mind consists of ideas and thoughts that are very much in our awareness, while the unconscious mind contains deeper, hidden thoughts, beliefs and emotions. Much of the unconscious mind is irrational, while the conscious mind is largely rational. The conscious and unconscious minds work together, for the most part, with conscious thoughts infiltrating the unconscious and vice versa. Interestingly, even though we think we are aware and highly conscious, the mind and consciousness itself remains mysterious.

The mind, as a whole, has the task of making sense and discriminating between what is appropriate and 'real' for each of us. Although we can become aware of what is in our conscious mind, through personal reflection, interactions with others, counselling or coaching, or in many other ways, we may be quite unaware, of what is in our unconscious mind. Until we notice the patterns running through our lives. While we all welcome good patterns, we know that destructive patterns can cause havoc in our personal, relational or financial lives, unless they are can be addressed and changed.

The existence of the unconscious mind in the human psyche is now largely accepted and is no longer contested by the majority of the educated populations of the world, including the medical fields. However, this general acceptance of the existence of the unconscious mind, or unconscious elements, brings up some interesting dilemmas, if we consider what this means.

In considering whether we have one or more lives, if it is true that we have only one life, then it would follow that we would be born as empty vessels with clear, clean minds, much like a brand new computer with an empty hard disk or backup drive. However, this appears not to be the case. Consider newborn babies. Some appear to be born angry, while others are sad, anxious or calm right from the first breath. How is this so, if we are all arriving for the first time into one life, as an empty vessel?

If we look at the work of psychiatrist, B. Weiss (1988) in *Many Lives, Many Masters*, he, contrary to the beliefs of the psychiatric profession, educationalists and culture, found that many of his patients, when hypnotised, went back to former lives to find the source of their mental health problems. We can see that Weiss's discoveries through his work have joined many others, to provide a growing body of information that could be claimed to be evidence of reincarnation. R. Webster (2001) in *Past Life Memories* has also added to the growing wealth of evidence for the existence of more than one life by recording former lives that clients' accessed during hypnosis. Webster was able to go even further by verifying some of the information collected in hypnotic trance with hard, factual and historical evidence that was published in his book as proof of the validity of past life experiences.

Further, R. Bullivant (2012) in *12 Real Life Reincarnation and Past Lives in the News: Global Evidence of Reincarnation and Past Lives*, provides details of further valuable examples for exploration. However, even though there is a growing body of 'evidence' for the existence of past lives by such historical verification that is hard to explain otherwise, many of the past life experiences recorded cannot be verified. In reality, the belief of being involved in a cycle of rebirth goes back a long way, although it ultimately remains a choice as to whether we believe it or not. Both Weiss and Bullivant provide a lot of evidence challenging the idea that if we have one life only, such memories, some of which may be verified, would not be possible.

If we have one life, our minds would start off as clear with no imprints of former existences at all. However, if we do have more than one life or even a series of lives, it makes sense that some of us are born fearful or anxious, while others are born passive, even within one family with the same genetic imprint and the same home and cultural conditioning. In light of this, the fact that we have an unconscious mind and that much of our involuntary behaviour and feelings come from this, we begin to gain some insight about the complexity of the human expereince. The idea that the mind stores up all of our experiences, without discrimination, and appears to be a mixture of present life and other experiences, is very interesting. The question still remains though: how is it that babies are born happy, fearful or sad if they all come into the world for the first and only time? The theory of reincarnation has been lost in the mists of time although it is seeing a revival.

The oldest record of the belief in reincarnation is found in the Indian manuscript, *The Bhagavad-Gita*.

> *"Bhagavad-Gita, is thousands of years older than the Dead Sea Scrolls, provides the most complete explanation of reincarnation available anywhere. Since spiritual knowledge is eternally true and does not change with each new scientific theory."*
> From *Coming Back AC*. Bhaktivedanta Swami Prabhupada, p xv (1995).

Perhaps, in reality, the cycle of death and rebirth is present both within each life, as well as between lives. Life and death takes place within us constantly and in the universe. The cells of our bodies are constantly dying and being reformed on a moment by-moment basis, so that every seven years or so our whole body is renewed. Of course, we only need to look at the cycles of nature and the universe, such as day and night, the waxing and waning of the moon and the flow of the seasons, and so much more beyond our planetary cycles, to realise that we are part of a natural order. One that is bigger than all of us.

We can see life and death through the fact that solar systems come into being as others collapse. As they are all locked into a cycle of creation and destruction, why shouldn't we too be involved in a cycle of rebirth? A soul might live on and simply move into another body at physical death, in order to continue the experience of living, just like everything in the universe that is involved in the cycle of creation and destruction. Much of what we have in our unconscious minds may indeed come from this life, as the unconscious mind stores up all experiences and may be traced back to earlier times in our lives or childhoods. However, there is also much that makes no sense in our present experience, such as our fears and anxieties that are often totally out of step with the real life events and situations of our present life. According to Bullivant, some people hold a level of trauma in their psyche that has no bearing in their lives that appear to have no known traumatic events. However, the roots of some experiences may be traced back to former lives or former generations, through such processes as hypnotherapy or systemic processes, such as family constellations (to be discussed later). These can often be resolved here in the life of the person concerned with the use of good therapeutic processes.

British poet laureate, John Masefield wrote:

> *I hold that when a person dies*
> *His soul returns again to Earth:*
> *Arrayed in some new flesh disguise,*
> *Another mother gives him birth*
> *With sturdier limbs and a brighter brain*
> *The old soul takes the road again.*
> Coming Back AC. Bhaktivedanta Swami Prabhupada, p xi (1995).

The idea that we have lived before enables us to account for the store of innate wisdom or knowledge that many of us carry with us and, hence, contributes to our power to create our reality. Let's consider that thoughts create reality. In fact, what we expect is what we create, according to C. J. Jenson (2012) in *Writings of Dr Joseph Murphy*. He goes to great lengths to explain how this works and how this knowledge may be used to empower us. Moreover, J. Robertson (2011) in *The Seth Books, The Nature of Personal Reality*, is a classic source of knowledge concerning the nature of the mind to explain our power to create reality from our thoughts. This means that our thoughts, whether they are conscious or unconscious, have the power to create our reality, and do so constantly. Conscious thoughts and beliefs formed in this life, as well as remnants of beliefs, experiences or expectations from past lives or former generations, may imprint potent messages on the unconscious mind. It is the nature of the unconscious mind to have no discrimination. Therefore, it does not know what is real or not, good or bad, hence, the mixed up nature of our thoughts and dreams. There is no doubt that the unconscious elements of our minds have an impact on how we create our realities.

On the other hand, a perception that is freely formed from experience, that is not coming from past lives or the unconscious mind, also has the power to form expectations, thoughts, beliefs and, hence, a reality. There is no difference between good or bad and accurate or inaccurate perceptions, from the mind's perspective. The mind or consciousness simply doesn't know what the effects are going to be of what it is creating, for the most part, until our wisdom increases through lived experiences of wisdom. Wisdom is developed by deep learnings form lived experiences.

In addition, much of what we create may come from the unconscious mind and may only be seen and assessed when the effects of is, is seen in patterns that are created that can be felt or experienced in concrete terms. We can see the patterns as they have played out in our lives. Often we create whatever is in our mind without knowing how, until we begin to notice what we are bringing into concrete form over and over again. Only when we have seen this often enough can we become more aware of how we form our reality. Interestingly, in this process, even though awareness is wonderful, it is only the first step towards making positive change.

We create our realities from our thoughts and feelings.

These come from our:

1. Conscious mind, thoughts, beliefs and feelings
2. Unconscious mind hidden thoughts, beliefs and feelings.

By raising your awareness, if a reality or pattern is negative, then you can change it by changing the underlying problematic thought or belief. By making changes, you can indeed change your reality. The purpose of this book is to give you the knowledge and the tools to take mastery of your own life to become rich and spiritual, consciously.

If we consider the soul's journey from a reincarnation perspective, in the beginning, the soul is pure and perfect in its innocence and ignorance that is hungry for experiences. We may picture such a pure, new soul as translucent in colour. The soul undergoes a transformation due to the impact of experiences. However, over time, due to wear and tear, success, happiness and also difficult experiences, a mixed reality is created. We may imagine the soul is now as a more mottled colour.

In addition, difficult experiences that perhaps couldn't be processed, may be held onto as trapped, unresolved and traumatic emotions. They lie trapped in the body, energy centres and the unconscious mind, seeking expression or release. These can be projected outwards in experiences of disappointment, stress, fear and anguish. Such residual emotions may form the basis of unhealthy beliefs and tainted expectations. Such unconscious feelings and experiences become the realities we create.

Interestingly, each time a belief is formed, we think it's true. The only way we can test it out is to live it; try it out to see if it is what we want and makes us happy. Of course, we are all looking for happiness, ultimately.

On another level, for immeasurable amounts of time, we may hold onto many unhelpful beliefs and distressed emotions on the soul journey.

Imagine that, over many lives, our original translucent soul becomes muddier in colour as we experience more. Through many mixed experiences, we accumulate many more convoluted beliefs and feelings in our search for the love and happiness that we know is there somewhere, as we continue to create our reality. We feel compelled to pursue each belief and live it out to its final outcome, in order to experience the consequence of what we have created. Only through this can we seriously come to a point where we can start to question what we are creating and begin to understand the validity or not of our beliefs and feelings. Through this process, we can come to realise that, just because we think our beliefs or feelings are valid, it does not necessarily make them so.

Only many lives of experiences can eventually give us the wisdom to realise what we are doing to ourselves through our freedom to create. This eventually matures into wisdom. Wisdom is the transformation of hard-earned experiences into a deep inner knowing that is in line with cosmic law. Gradually, through many experiences, we adjust or discard unhelpful beliefs in favour of healthier ones, and the murkiness around the soul begins to clear again, but this time with the glow of wisdom that has been earned through experience. As we begin to release or resolve stuck emotional states and unhealthy beliefs, the murky layers can start to dissolve as the clarity of the soul re-emerges into view. Now we can begin to appreciate who and what we really are.

Yes, we are perfect and special, but not in the way we may have imagined initially. Our soul is perfect, but because of the experience of separation on our entry into the physical world and the inception of the struggle to discover who we are in so many different ways. We take on or create many beliefs that we eventually discover do not make us happy. We suffer traumas and disappointments that, along with our beliefs, keep us stuck in difficult cycles and patterns. This keeps creating difficult realities for us.

Eventually, when we've had enough of the trauma, disappointments and struggle, we seek to find ways to let go of stuck emotions and create beliefs that may bring happiness. This entails refining and purifying our beliefs and emotions until they are in synchronicity with our soul. In this way, we find harmony in reconnecting with ourselves and the universal energy, as spiritual beings. From this point on, we can start the process of bringing the body, mind and soul together to come back into 'oneness'. We are indeed special, like the perfection of a snowflake or a drop of water; unique and yet much like all others. We are not above or below anyone else. We are equal and special, as are all souls.

Here, I invite you to take part in an exercise of goal development that will start now and continue throughout this book.

Consider one goal. Notice if you are struggling to find one or need to choose one from many. If you don't have a goal now, it may become more apparent as you go through this book. For those who have a goal, focus on it and write it down.

Notice how you feel when you envision having achieved it. Go back to this vision and feeling frequently throughout your day.

There are many levels of consciousness.

CHAPTER 5

Our Dilemma: Expansion of the Natural Order

We are individuals and also very much a part of society. By wanting to become rich and spiritual, there are natural as well as rigid societal forces in place. The planet and the universe are abundant, prolific, creative and wildly impulsive. There is an impulse in all things to expand, take seed and multiply. Look at how easily weeds continually raise their heads, or how the vast array of species of living things form and reform over time, and expand and go forth as conditions allow. Of course, each movement of growth is accompanied by withdrawals and extinctions too, over time, and as conditions change, the life force continues on relentlessly in one way or another. Hence, we know about the end of the dinosaur era and other extinct species, as newer ones constantly come forth to take their place. Nature is abundant, the planet is abundant and so is the universe. They and we are all part of cycles within cycles being driven by an incessant creative life force that knows no boundaries.

We are an integral part of nature, life force and the creative forces of the universe, and we are blessed with consciousness. Our task in the material world is to discover and master our creativity and there is no reason why the journey of the discovery, in itself, should not be enjoyable too. The physicality of our existence means that we are posed with the task of mastering our abilities to create our place in the world and make it pleasurable or otherwise. We do this through our actions and eventually we begin to notice that our intentions and thoughts are potent forces for how we live.

Now we come to some interesting ideas that, to my knowledge, were first posed by Wattles in the early 1920s as seen in the (2007 edition). He said that by addressing the notion of creative energy, the universe is permeated by an invisible substance that he explains is formless energy. This is the source of all creation and manifestation; pure creative potential that only requires to be imprinted by intention or thought forms in order to become reality. I will call this life force 'neutral matter'. Neutral matter permeates all matter and the spaces in-between. If life force through neutral matter can't express itself through one form, it does so through another, appearing to have no preference, as long as it can take form, as is shown in nature. Form is its natural expression.

We are part of the abundance of the planet and the universe. We come from it and go back to it in death. Like a flower in bloom, in all our glory, we shine and grow as tall and as healthy as we can with the available resources, before inevitably becoming part of the figurative compost that sustains the next thrust into life. And so it continues, cycles within cycles.

Nature is in us, just as we are in nature; a part of the energy of the cosmos. There are no limitations, as we are part of 'All That Is'. We are part of creative energy and, possibly, one of the latest expressions of life force and we have consciousness; a mind, vision, imagination and desire. Desire is on our first breath and an integral part of being human and part of life force. We are born out of the exuberance of life force and neutral energy, and are part of the creative energy of the universe and it is part of us.

Each of us already create our realities with our actions and in other ways too. We have consciousness, will and desire and, once we have mastered the art of survival and are in tune with our creative forces, we are much like the life force of the cosmos. Therefore, it is natural that we feel an impulse to expand our experiences. As human beings, we are openly desirous of more. Just as life force knows no limitations and is constantly going forth, pushing at the boundaries of what is possible, so too is our natural impulse for experiences of all kinds.

Interestingly, in order to experience more in this physical plane, it is necessary to have sufficient resources or wealth to be able to afford to pursue our desires and follow our impulses. It is necessary to have the resources to enable us to explore our desires if we are to follow our natural impulses for expansion and abundance. Of course, we require a lucrative currency to enable us to acquire and enjoy abundance in this material environment. That is the way this physical world is set up. First we need to master survival and then we can follow our desire for expansion through comforts, growth and enjoyment of all kinds. This requires the acquisition of currency so that we can barter. Barta is how we give and receive on the planet. So, if this is so natural, what is it that gets in the way of being able to create and receive abundance, and become rich?

To find some answers, let's look at the world.

The world and the planet, including the environment, is the stage on which we live. The world includes our social, cultural and political experiences, which are human-made. The planet Earth is the physical environment where we exist, and it is made up of the physical elements of air, water and land. The natural environment is the delicate evolving equilibrium of living forces at play that support life, if appropriate conditions are maintained. Regardless of the reasons for us being here, which is something that many of us may never be able to understand fully in this body, mind and place, we find ourselves born into a complex social, political, financial and religious web of human-made realities as well.

There are many human structures, ideas and expectations woven throughout the fabric of our families and societies. Such structures have many functions for us personally and collectively, by giving us a sense of belonging and cohesion in community. Structural provide us with social codes by which we may be encouraged into safety and order. Such social systems also provide structures that help us know our place in society, so much so, that there is often an unspoken expectation (often contrary to legislation that supports equality for all, in many countries) that individuals act in accordance with their station in life and agree to not 'rock the boat,' by rising beyond the station of our origins. Don't become too different to your group, Thereby remaining connected and don't upset the societal expectations of us. There is a belief that people operating outside social norms cause havoc by upsetting the societal order and challenge those in power. This has been the case for a long time but, at this time in history, many social barriers are being challenged. For many reasons, there is a merge taking place between cultures, races and gender, in a way that has never happened before. Many of us are challenging our place in society and societal expectations, and searching for new meaning. So, we are a part of, and in the process of creating new realities for ourselves in our world.

Religion and Self-Sacrifice

In terms of spirituality, there has traditionally been a notion of aspiration or admiration towards icons, such as Mother Theresa or Mahatma Gandhi (powerful symbols of spirituality or religiosity). So much so that it has become a common belief to expect that true spirituality should involve self-sacrifice as an essential element that proves authenticity. This is compounded by many stories in a range of religious texts around the world, promoting the virtues of self-sacrifice, poverty and simplicity for ordinary people. This is often in direct contrast to the wealth and entitlement that is often enjoyed by the ruling classes, including the clergy. Here we have the roots of some of the ideas that have permeated mass consciousness for thousands of years. There is often an assumption particularly by religious orders the public being sinful and unworthy. So much so that they were not worthy of a direct connection or relationship with their creator. Hence, humanity is often born into an assumed mass consciousness of guilt and unworthiness, that is largely upheld by major world religions, politics and society, that serves to maintain control and power by those in charge.

This resulted in an assumption that the role of the vast majority of the masses was to serve the higher classes of society. This was entrenched in tradition, political power and enforced by religion, into beliefs that ordinary people don't have the potential or moral right to attempt to improve their station in life. That to do so indicates that such people are selfish and should feel guilt.

Then a back swing of thinking in business sectors took place, known as the 'greed is good' movement. This started in the late 1980s and is still current in neo-liberal politics and the corporate and financial fields of the present.

> *"Greed, for lack of a better word, is good. Greed is right. Greed works. Greed clarifies, cuts through and captures, and is the essence of the evolutionary spirit. Greed, in all its forms; greed for life, for money, for love and knowledge, has marked the upward surge of mankind and greed, you mark my words, will not only save Teldar Paper, but that other malfunctioning corporation called the USA."*
> Gekko (1987)

Here we have a glimpse of our dilemma.

To be rich is to want more and to take and enjoy more of what the world has to offer. Traditionally, being religious or spiritual has meant that you are satisfied or happy with less or very little. These are the psychological structures and beliefs that are deeply entrenched in individuals and in mass consciousness. These structures must be broken down, refined, adjusted or discarded and new ones built, if we are to see that it is possible, desirable and NATURAL to be Rich AND Spiritual. Rich AND

Spiritual together, so that we may be abundant in attracting and receiving what we want in our own unique way, and in a way that is both unlimited and guiltless.

We are in the process of experiencing great change in our world at this time, where strongly held traditions and beliefs are dissolving, as new financial, social and technological developments rise. We are having to redefine many of our ideas and desires, as we create our realities more consciously. Humanity has gone through many phases of growth and development. At present, we are in the grip of the 'greed is good' era; 'dog eats dog', 'winners and losers', 'domination and submission', 'wealth and poverty', to name only a few. For many people on this planet, there are only two choices: take all or become a loser. Compete and annihilate all others to win at any cost. Wealth has become so synonymous with this conquering and annihilating attitude, that many of us feel an inner repulsion towards joining them in aspiring for wealth. There is often a feeling of discomfort when taking more for yourself because this is often perceived as being directly linked to taking from or depriving others in some way.

This is often upheld by deep societal and personal belief systems. Feeling guilty or greedy is not at all how any of us want to feel and so, for many of us, we prefer to avoid wealth and secretly chastise ourselves and others for wanting more. It's natural that we don't want to become like those with whom we are not in moral alignment. In addition, there may also be a feeling of disloyalty when swapping elegancies from those of the poor to the wealthy. Particularly if we have a deeply felt loyalty to those who are struggling.

Many of us have the feeling of not being able to enjoy wealth in the face of so much poverty or suffering in the world. This is commonly due to having a family history that involves stories of suffering, poverty and hardship. Hence, we have conscious or often hidden repulsions towards the idea of wealth, because it does not fit in well with our historic, ethical, moral or spiritual aspirations. It may not fit in with our traditional religious ideas of the need for self-sacrifice, or with spiritual ideas we may have of equality, compassion and generosity for all. All of these thoughts and feelings can pull us away from becoming rich. These deeply held and often hidden beliefs may become our saboteurs or blocks to wealth and are often subconscious.

If we look at the natural world, it is easy to see that there is enough for everyone and that there are solutions to the problems of the world, if we would only collectively raise our consciousness to find creative answers. It is a fact that most of the wealth of the world is owned by a very small percentage of people. We are in the grip of financial institutions and human-made unsustainable structures of finance, such as the stock market. These structures are inextricably linked to the capitalist ideals of democracy that fail, in terms of justice and human compassion, to provide an even playing field for all nations and races. Equality and fairness is not part of an agenda that is run by vested interests and greed. Interestingly, the health of the environment is also often NOT taken into consideration in such worldly matters. The quality and health of the most vital elements necessary to sustain us on our planet, such as air, water, food and the health of the landscape, are simply not part of the tally of considerations valued as important enough, to be included in the financial index or the financial structures of the world.

The human-made structures of such institutions as the financial structures of the world, in general, are so disconnected from the state of the natural planet, that they don't include the impact of the human race of the natural environment. There is no consideration of the human impact on natural resources and the destruction of the equilibrium of the natural cycles on which we all depend, for life. Water, food, soil and forests and their health seemingly have no value. At this time, the world is largely run by economists who have a blinkered view of what needs to be considered as important. Where profit alone is the only measure of success. Many people have become rich through this system. However, this way of becoming rich is not sustainable, either in stock market terms, or in the treatment of the planet, because it leaves consideration of the essential elements of life on the planet out of the equation. We are embodied creatures and we and our children and grandchildren require the elements of water, air and the climate to be in a healthy, balanced state, for survival.

The world is run in a deeply destructive and competitive way.

The current economy and business in general is based on a belief in competition. This is a culture of winning and losing, with the winner taking all and having ultimate power. Limitation and scarcity is built into this way of thinking. However, this is old thinking that has brought us to the brink of where we are now, and it is crumbling. In order to grow rich and still maintain spirituality, there is a need for a new attitude. That of cooperation, rather than competition.

In reality, if you believe that the world is abundant, there is no need for an attitude of competition. There is enough for everyone, particularly if you are creative with your intentions in choosing cooperation rather than competition as your strategy of choice. You can go into roles of work that are vacant or have not yet been formed. You can go into business in ways that are unique and attract customers who are attracted to your way of thinking in innovation or growing your business. If you have the intention of being in full cooperation with creative forces, you can be at the forefront of new thoughts and ways of working, creating wealth in a cooperative way that harms no one. Look how Facebook, an extremely creative idea, was developed with little finance. It has manifested its own market using the power of cooperation. There was no need for competition with such a new idea because it was unique. I know that having become part of the status quo such groups as Facebook are now wielding their own power, but the innovation and creativity of their formation remains and may be admired. How we deal with success is the real test of being rich and spiritual.

Even if you are in an industry much like many others, as I am, you can find ways to be different or unique to attract only those clients and colleagues who are happy to come to you and will benefit from working with you, in your way. There are enough customers for every business that has something good to offer. In this way, each business can become abundant, according to their own ability to be clear, focussed and creative.

When moving from competition to cooperation in the formulation of your intentions, thoughts and actions, simply turn your focus to cooperation with natural forces and supportive people. A synchronicity of the energies of human intention with the natural environment. In this way, you can attract those who will benefit from what you offer, and so everyone wins.

Don't focus on competition unless you want that in your life. In a competitive world, you may be the winner today, but inevitably, you will eventually become the loser.

When you have an attitude of abundance and cooperation, it is always beneficial to be generous with your services and in the treatment of others. Make sure that you always fulfill your obligations generously, while maintaining an efficient, professional and business-like attitude. Stinginess has no place in an abundant field of manifestation because it would spoil the focus on neutral matter, making it less potent. If you employ people, be fair; if you sell your services, give a good measure to ensure satisfaction without selling yourself short. There is a way to be generous so as to keep the flow of 'give and take' running healthily and generously in your life, as you reap abundance.

For these reasons, to change your own situation or attitude to that of being rich and spiritual, you may need to change your mind-set in several ways. You will need to create your own reality and align yourself with others of a similar mindset, where possible, so as to new streams of reality. This will enable you to live more abundantly and create within a creative world for your own delight.

If it is not possible to align yourself with others at this time, then you must do it by yourself initially, and frequently you will find similar energies to align with.

You are being invited to come out of your conditioning and form a new reality: a reality that is yours and fits in easily with your spirituality, ethics and desire to be abundant. Sound easy? Yes, on one level it is, but it may take time to let go of old patterns of conditioning and thinking. However, the speed of this process itself depends on how much you want it and are ready for change.

Our creator, God, universal energy or 'All That Is', is in agreement with each of us creating our own reality and becoming rich and spiritual. It is my belief that this is what we are here for. If I hold that belief, it becomes part of my reality and part of what I am creating.

For those people who are sceptical and hold an opposite belief, they will create and experience a different reality. We can only test the validity of our beliefs through our experiences of life. Generally, those who expect struggle, often struggle and those who know about the prolific abundance of the universe, are often prolifically abundant. This is part of the spiritual experiment or experience we are involved in, to discover who we are as human beings. We have a choice and it is a great adventure.

The human-made world, as we know it, has already been formed by the visions of those in power and for their ultimate desire for control and wealth over others, often at any cost. We can continue as we are, being run by present mass consciousness and the structures created by those in power, or we can take our power back and live in our own image, in abundance. Be aware that by continuing as we are, we are supporting the status quo, silently.

On another level, the world is perfect as it is. We are all a product of it and have benefitted from it and are part of the present mass consciousness, without exception. It has brought us to a point where we can question and explore ourselves in the world. It is perhaps a perfect place for us to experiment with our own creative powers and discover ourselves. We can test our beliefs and actions in this reality, to see what consequences unfold, and we can do so constantly. We can begin to define ourselves and create other realities as we realise and utilise our creative power. We have unlimited choice once we step into our freedom.

As I have previously mentioned, the universe is abundantly prolific. This idea is not new, as W. Wattle (2013), first edition, 1910 and N. Hill (2012), whose first edition was in 1937, both explain in their own ways. There is a natural and innate movement towards prosperity in men and women. Wattle and Hill both noticed how successful people do what they do, to provide examples for us in our quest for becoming rich.

Consider the following:

Do you believe that you can only be happy being wealthy in a world where there is fairness and justice?

Yes ____ No ____

Do you believe that you can only agree to be rich if those around you are also rich?

Yes ____ No ____

Consider your goal and how you feel about it now, in light of the dilemma we all face, in terms of traditional, social and religious conditioning.

Reflect on what impact, if any, these beliefs have had, or are having on how you feel about your goal.

Abundance is natural

CHAPTER 6

A Metaphor for Life: Fullness

How we experience our reality has a big effect on how we create our life and our attitude to wealth and spirituality. Human reality is subjective (open to individual interpretation) and we are all challenged with the task of making meaning of our experiences. As human beings, we are primed to make sense; to understand the reason for our existence through our senses and experience. This becomes our reality. Experience is subjective. It's interesting to note how a group of people who go through the same experience may each have a different perception of it. This is why, even in the same family, each sibling can have a different view of their childhood, even though Mum, Dad and the environment were the same. They each experience it from a slightly different standpoint, with each having a slightly or even a very different experience and, hence, often forming a different memory. From our perception we make meaning of ourselves, others and situations. We are not driven by the actual facts, but by the perceptions we have of our experiences.

From Experience to Perception

From experiences we make assumptions and expectations that are influential in becoming part of our world view. For example, some people see the world as a scary place, while others experience it as safe. We all live in the same world. Many view a glass with water in it as, half-full, while others see it as half-empty and yet it's the same glass of water.

It seems that those people who view the glass as half-empty have experiences that did not turn out well. Or were traumatic and violent. Many people come from families that have a troubled and heavy destiny that have resulted in them taking a half-empty (negative) view of the world. People with this view choose to look for the downside of situations, perhaps to shelter themselves from disappointment, because it is their experience that things don't work out so well.

The problem with this is if your a glass-half-empty person, you are putting this out into your world. With this expectation it is unlikely that you will notice any golden opportunities that come your way. Interestingly, some people who haven't had any major misfortune or trauma in their lives but still have a glass half empty perception on life.

Alternatively, there are others in the world who have experienced adversity and tragedy in their lives, and still manage to maintain a glass-half-full attitude. They choose to find a gem of wisdom or learning from experiences and then are able to process so they could let it go and move on, richer from their experiences. Yes, there is nature and nurture, but there is also choice.

So, perhaps at the end of the day, being conscious of which attitude you adopt is important so as to be aware of how you create your reality.

While many of us may wish we'd had a more settled and easy transition through life, in reality, there are advantages and disadvantages to having either a challenging or easier life experience. In the end, it is you who chooses how you perceive.

In my experience as a therapist, many people who have had a nurturing and secure upbringing, are frequently less able to cope well with adversity, because their life experience has not prepared them for unexpected downturns. They haven't had the opportunities to build resilience into their personality.

This is often in direct contrast to some who've had more difficult experiences of life and have somehow managed to process it, build more resilience and make different choices in the way they approach life.

Regardless of your life experiences, there are challenges involved with having an easier or alternatively, a tougher life, because it's up to you how you perceive it.

If you reflect on yourself, you will notice your propensity to optimism or pessimism in your thoughts and words. Most of us come from mixed situations as we all come from complex levels of generational patterns. A rich background of experiences from which to create our perceptions.

Very few of us have a 'perfect' upbringing. What is perfect anyway?

I have a large Buddha in my house who is bowing deeply into his hands. Some people perceive him as weeping, while others see him bowing in gratitude. Again, glass-half-empty or glass half-full. This way of thinking comes out in everything.

Notice your natural inclination and then reflect on whether you choose to stay with it, or realise that it might be wise change it.

The good news is that you are free to make a choice. You can change your original world view or perception at any time you wish, if you find that your present view is not in your best interests.

- Reflect on whether you are generally optimistic or pessimistic.
- Remember, your views are yours, because they come from you and only you can change them.
- Are you a glass-half-full or glass-half-empty person?

To be able to attract wealth into your life, you need to be able to visualise a better future, so having an optimistic outlook is vital if you want to be rich.

Consider your goal. If you can still feel it or see it clearly, that is great. However, if you find it hard to hold onto or visualise, reflect on this in terms of whether you view life through a half-full or half-empty glass.

A full glass leads to a full life.

CHAPTER 7

Acceptance

Acceptance is an important first step in wealth creation.

Acknowledging What Is (1999), by Bert Hellinger, and *Loving What Is* (2002), by Byron Katie, both emphasise the importance of acceptance and the ability to acknowledge and accept reality. Accept reality just as it is, as a starting point in any situation in life. So too is acknowledging reality and loving What Is, is important in being rich and spiritual. This is because it includes being able to acknowledge What Is, knowing it's not in your personal power to change. This may be history itself, or situations that simply Are, or other peoples' choices and their consequences. Unfortunately, many people are stuck in looking back. Focussed on what has already taken place that can't be changed. Spending time feeling frustrated about not being able to alter the attitudes or actions of others, or regretting personal choices.

Anyone spending too much time doing this is literally, spending their life, (valuable time), energy and feelings in looking back.

Alternatively, others stay too focussed on the future. Being stuck in the past or focussing too much on the future is not only a waste of time, and time is literally your life. It's also a waste of energy. This is a misuse of the power of focus, that could be used in a much more productive way, in creation, so you could be rich and spiritual.

Let's consider acceptance. Acceptance shows an attitude of realism. The ability to be fully focussed on the present and not being drawn to the past or overly concerned or fearful of the future. Of course, we do need to look back sometimes to make sense of what happened, but only to take into the present the gems of learning or wisdom it offers. It is also necessary to plan the future, but having done that, there is a need to return to the present. With this attitude, it is possible to focus clearly on having a reality in the present.

Acceptance is a deep and complex state. It means the acceptance of life up to the point of NOW. If you are constantly replaying the past or wallowing in thoughts or feelings about it, you are not accepting it, or moving on. Acceptance means taking full unconditional responsibility for yourself up to this point in time. Of course, this includes all of the gaffs, poor choices and difficult situations you have created, or were caused by the choices of others. It includes all the positive and less positive decisions and actions taken in your life.

In reality, it is a fact that you would not be who you are now without EVERYTHING that has happened so far in your life. ALL of it has shaped you. If you can come to this point of acceptance, you can use all of your experiences from the past and your presence in the NOW to move forward in your life. If the past has been painful, the only choices to be made are to either change your perception of it, or to stay with the pain. It is your choice to move on and take the jewel of wisdom from the experience. If you are not able to find the wisdom at this time, then just accept the facts of what happened and the reality that you are here now, safe.

There is a need to realise what has happened in the past and change any negative perception of it into something more positive, so you can learn from it. Importantly, you are in charge of what happens NOW. Focussing on what is in your control is empowering, whereas focussing on what is done, gone or lost, is disempowering, unless you can find a lesson, or a gift from the situation.

If you can't do it by yourself seek effective help. By dealing with the past, you can take any positive lessons from it and acknowledge any negative aspects that you don't want to repeat. Of course, you can also make amends or offer an apology to others, if appropriate, but you can't force others to do likewise. The past can't be undone; we don't have control over others and neither should we.

If you look at the past from the aspect of its potential to inform, you can gain something positive from the experience. It can form part of the nutrients from which you may grow further; for now and into the future. Even learning what NOT to do in the present or future, as a result of events in your life, is a positive lesson. From here, you can move towards acceptance and, perhaps you will eventually be able to thank the situation for its gift of transformation, truth or guidance it has given you.

Alternatively, you can hold grudges, vent anger or hate at yourself or others, or even God, for the rest of your life. This is to become stuck in a cycle of negativity, constantly giving away personal power. This must surely be hell.

You have a choice. Whatever has happened has already taken place. You can accept it, rage against it, or become depressed about it. Hard though this might seem, it's a choice that only you can make. Alternatively, you can resign yourself to it, in a poor me attitude.

Acceptance is not resignation. However, resignation may be one of the steps that lead to acceptance. For example, where someone is born with a disability, or into difficult life circumstances, these situations are challenging, as is a death, the end of a relationship or a career. Such events may be resisted, raged against or mourned and, through choice, can eventually lead to acceptance. Anger, sadness and grief are normal emotions to be felt for a while before being processed and let go of, prior to acceptance. Alternatively, such feelings may be held onto and used as reasons for not being successful, not having good relationships, or the reason for living in poverty. Here, the person falls into a victim mentality.

Acceptance is accepting 'what is'. This means saying 'yes' to your place in the universe; accepting the life you are living. 'Yes' opens the door to new possibilities and 'no' is the dark hole of denial and depression.

Accepting yourself and your life just as it is, requires the letting go of ego, which can be a humbling and also a spiritual experience. This is unconditional acceptance. If you find yourself saying, 'but what about this, or that', or feeling that you have been dealt a poor hand, or been treated badly, you are not yet experiencing unconditional acceptance. If you can eventually come to acceptance, this is a new starting point; the beginning of a new perspective on life.

Coming to acceptance can be a long journey for some. However, it is vital to come to a good place in this, in order to take the next step towards richness and spirituality. Acceptance is affirmative; a positive impulse towards life and a place from which you can make choices, whereas resignation is a withdrawal from life. However, resignation may well be a vital step before the movement towards acceptance for many.

In reality, we all go through crises, adversity, trauma and misfortune. We all experience the full spectrum of life from joy, excitement and happiness to sadness, anger, shame and guilt, and it is HOW we cope and perceive both the positive and negative events of our life that is important. This shows the depth of our wisdom and spirituality.

One woman I know, who was sexually abused, was able to process what had happened to her with a little help and has moved on successfully in her life, while another, who was also sexually abused and received extensive help and therapy, has not managed to take back her power or been able to move on, and still blames the abuse for her inability to have a relationship or career, many years later.

Jack lost his long-term partner to cancer and is still in the throes of deep grief, ten years later. He still feels angry, depressed and sad over his loss, while Susan, after one year of grieving her husband's death, was able to move on to the next phase in her life. She still thinks of him and sheds tears, always keeps his photo close at hand and often tells warm stories of their time together.

Acceptance

Some people manage to find acceptance and a new perspective, while others do not. Somehow, some of us have more resilience and ability to process shock, grief or loss than others and, hence, also have the ability to let it go and move on. Many people have the ability and willingness to come to a place of acceptance of what happened and are able to find a new perspective, while some people do not. This seems crucial to their success in living and, of course, becoming rich and spiritual. This ability to be resilient, accepting and find a new perspective is vital. So too, in wealth creation, is the capacity to accept situations as they are and find new healthy perspectives that are required to being fully present in the NOW and open to new possibilities.

Being able to accept a setback, disadvantage or restriction and stay focussed on a better present and future, is a necessary attribute to creating a better future and becoming rich. Look at the lives of people like Aung San Suu Kyi, the Burmese, nonviolent social-justice fighter who has spent many years under house arrest, and the Dalai Lama, who is exiled from his beloved homeland of Tibet, due to its invasion by China. These are two shining examples of people not only surviving, but growing through adversity and demonstrating acceptance and an ability to form new perspectives with resilience and optimism.

A complex part of the wisdom of acceptance is an ability to come to a realisation of what can't be changed, must be accepted and what is in your power to change. This clarity, when applied, is an important asset and an essential part of becoming rich, as it is to all areas of life. If you focus on your goal, in the present, it doesn't diminish, weaken or waste your energy, on what is byond your control.

Jenny was a contractor who worked for a big corporate body that was constantly going through reform and downsizing of the workforce. She also had a small business that she was developing in her spare time. Jenny was so distressed with the constant changes and the lack of management consultation with the workforce, that she decided she would leave as soon as she could. Upon seeing her a few months later, I was surprised to find that she was still working at the same place. When I asked her what had happened, she said that it was fine now because she had changed her perspective on the situation. She realised that, in many ways, this job, even as it was still serving her purpose and so she would continue there while she was building her other business. She said that, once she had come to this perspective and stopped resisting the changes towards simply accepting them. Just as they are. She started to enjoy her job again, in a different way.

Neither the situation nor the job had changed. She had changed her perspective. She had decided to find thoughts or beliefs that made her happy, rather than hanging onto those that had kept her stuck in anger and resentment. She had decided to take control of herself, her thoughts and her emotions. She did all of this while keeping her long term focus in mind. Using this job to allow her to grow her new business.

Her corporate job serves a purpose. One that worked well for her for a while that she has since outgrown. It forms a way of transitioning into her new business. A win, win attitude.

Consider the setbacks you've had in your life and how you have responded to them.

Can you accept your life as it is?

Unconditional acceptance shows that you have faith in the powers that drive the universe and all in it. Have faith that you are at the right time and place and ready to co-create positively with creative energy.

Feel the level of acceptance you have and notice how your goal feels now.

Yes to life is acceptance.

CHAPTER 8

Wealth Readiness, Life Purpose

In order to be able to become rich and spiritual, it is necessary to be ready for wealth. You might say that you are absolutely ready for wealth, or you wouldn't be reading this book. Who would not want to be rich? Perhaps the real question is, how much do you want to be rich? Many of us want wealth creation to be easy and are not prepared for what may be required to make it happen. While it may not be necessary for all of us to have to work hard to create wealth, it may be essential that change takes place internally. Changes that drive our attitudes and actions and our awareness.

It is a reality that if what you are doing is working, you would already be rich. If this is not the case, there must be room for change.

Wealth readiness is not as simple as it sounds. As described in the earlier chapter, when Mary was hoping to win her Sydney waterfront home through *The Secret* and a lottery ticket, a lack of clarity was apparent. Mostly, but not always, it is necessary to have clarity about what you really want in order for it to take form and become a reality. If you take the time to reflect, you can begin to notice a theme of desires in your life that drive you forward. These may include areas that you feel driven to follow or be involved in. If you are aware of these desires, you are in touch with your life purpose.

Life purpose and desire are bedfellows. Life purpose is the theme that underpins and drives your life. Your purpose will be driven by desires that you want to fulfill, as is the wish for experiences that propel you forward. Desire is what perpetuates life and is at the core of our existence. If we consider that, at its inception, is the sexual act of our parents. It is from this desire that transfers to the physical, that provides us with our entry into the world. Of course, we also have to be in agreement with this manifestation at the level of the soul, in choosing these parents and circumstances of our entry. Even though we may have no conscious knowledge of it. I believe that for each of us to be here is a miracle in itself, involving divine synchronicities, seeded by desire that come into alignment, in order to guide each soul into existence.

From this point on, our life takes shape and is driven by our desires. The desires to climb mountains or enjoy food, seek excitement or higher knowledge, or have a prestigious career, are all driven by desire and are a part of our life purpose. Each person having their own unique life purpose. It is true that some of us are intent on becoming rich as a primary goal, while many of us have other goals that simply require adequate finances to pursue them. Many just need sufficient wealth or resources to pursue their desires and purpose. For many of us, becoming rich is a subsidiary goal in order to enable the fruition of our primary goals. Goals that involve fulfilling experiences of all kinds, such as travel, adventure, thrills and excitement, that require some wealth as a starting point. However, the first step to becoming rich and spiritual is to be able to connect with your deepest desires, because this is where your life purpose lies.

In these highly material times, many of us think that wealth alone is what will make us happy and, like Mary, we may latch onto other peoples' or society's perceived dreams of happiness, rather than accessing our own unique desires and life purpose to find what our soul seeks.

Unfortunately, many of us are disconnected from our life purpose and live primarily in our head, lacking the awareness of, and connection to our, body, feelings and the natural environment. This is further exacerbated by many of us living in highly technological environments, that are totally divorced from nature, in high-rise concrete jungles. This has led to many of us becoming aware of our disconnection. A disconnection that becomes so uncomfortable we become triggered into a search for reconnection with ourselves and the natural environment. It is generally true that humankind has largely moved away from the fundamentals of our roots, community and environment since the time of the industrial revolution. Leaving many on a quest to rediscover their connection to themselves and significant others. Many people are doing this through the New Age movement, metaphysics, ancient folklore, personal development and a reconnection with spirituality and nature.

The upsurge in spirituality is taking place at the same time as a turning away from the restrictions and perceived control of formal religions, in a search for new meaning. Alternatively, some people are reconnecting with formal religion, perhaps in a new way. There is an impulse towards finding meaning that is more satisfying and embracing of the exploration and utilisation of our innate, creative, human potential in our search for love and abundance.

Interestingly, this awakening is taking place in the midst of the chaos on our planet, resulting in the collapse of many traditional structures. Many areas of dissolution are happening with the breakdown of families and social groups, while simultaneously, an explosion in population is taking place. At the same time, there is a growing gap between the dichotomies of the rich and poor, starving and obese, war and peace and the displacement at an unprecedented rate.

In addition, we are faced with the effects that we are having on the planet, in terms of environmental issues that are becoming more apparent, such as global warming, along with the decimation of forests. Excessive amounts of carbon dioxide have reached unprecedented levels in our atmosphere as a result of our insane race to burn most of the Earth's reserves of fossil fuels in just a couple of hundred years. It is ironic that, at the same time, the very lungs of the planet are also being systematically felled. The forests that could save us from the effects of our destruction through their natural ability to neutralise increasing carbon dioxide levels, are being systematically cut down.

On another level, many of us are becoming lost in the distinction between different realities: that of technology, cyber space or intellectual pursuits, to mention a few, that often seemingly swallow us up if we don't keep our feet squarely on the ground. There is an increasing need to remain grounded, as a connection with the Earth is essential if we are to expand our horizons into new realms in a positive way. We need to maintain an awareness of our physicality while we grow and develop our abilities to create the realities we choose to live in.

There is currently an awakening for many people from the extreme craziness on the planet, with many of us yearning for a reconnection with ourselves, our humanity and the cosmos, in our search for peace, harmony and love. These issues are discussed in more detail in my first book, *Stardust on the Spiritual Path*, where I take you on a journey of the soul's journey from inception towards liberation through the perspectives of Vedic astrology, karma, relationships and family constellations.

By looking at our experiences from a more cosmic perspective, Deepak Chopra, in several of his books in recent years, describes the art and practice of Vedic astrology as a highly useful and influential tool for personal development. The use and study of Vedic astrology is a part of the healing arts of the Chopra Centre in America. In his introduction to Vedic astrology, Chopra states succinctly in a YouTube video, dated 30 Jan, 2013 (retrieved 13 July, 2013), that we are deeply connected to the cosmos. The macro (big picture) in the cosmos is reflected in each of us at a micro level. In this way, Chopra explains the validity of knowledge and describes the practice of Vedic astrology as a legitimate and valuable guidance tool for spiritual counselling. Chopra makes the point that we are all connected and part of the cosmos and that the time for our perceived separation is over, if we are to raise our levels of consciousness.

This brings us back to the idea that we are all equal. We are all made of the same stuff and come into being in the same way.

If this is the case, you may ask, how is it that some of us:

- have so much more wisdom and are more naturally gifted than others?
- appear to have so much more clarity, centeredness and focus than others?
- children have more natural wisdom than our parents?
- older people appear to have little wisdom, while others have an infinite well of knowing?

Genetics alone cannot answer these bigger questions, as can be shown when we look at ourselves within our families. Children are born into families in a seemingly haphazard manner, with some being very much like their parents and others appearing to be so different that they are perceived to be almost of another species. Some family members may appear to be so unlike the rest of their clan that they can only be conditioned by family, education and society, to a limited degree, as character 'will win out' anyway, regardless of genetics and conditioning. Character will come out to show itself in a positive or a negative manner, or somewhere in between, in its own unique way.

So, how is it that each of us are as we are? All fundamentally the same and yet expressing ourselves so differently.

Here we come to Vedic astrology, the cosmic map of consciousness. Vedic astrology (Jyotish) is ancient Indian astrology, which is a knowledge, art and practice that dates back through the mists of time, from 3,000-5,000 BC. It is an ancient spiritual science that is part of the Vedic tradition of the Indus Valley in India; a spiritual science that is a natural evolution from the practice of astronomy, by noticing the effects that cosmic movements have on individuals.

Now I am going to discuss the kind of people that are ready for wealth, from a Vedic perspective. Vedic philosophy forms the basis of where

Wattles (2007) drew aspects of his knowledge, so I will outline some of the main points here.

I am a Vedic astrologer who regularly gives readings and courses to help people understand their cosmic map: the Vedic astrology chart. This is a chart that shows the karmic patterns that each person is born into and is here to experience.

From a Vedic perspective, we seemingly separate from the 'universal energy of oneness' when we drop into this physical plane and enter a state of illusion, known as 'Maya', on the cycle of reincarnation. We lose the awareness of our 'oneness with all' as we embark on a great adventure over possibly hundreds or thousands of lives through the wheel of rebirth.

We are challenged to explore and eventually master our physical realms through four main areas of human experience. These are Dharma, Artha, Kama (this is NOT karma) and Moksha.

Dharma	Right action that is in line with cosmic law.
Artha	Wealth creation, the art of mastering and utilising the material aspects of living from survival to abundance.
Kama	Desire for growth and adventures of all kinds.
Moksha	Enlightenment, an awakening and a return to the state of 'oneness' in human form and the end of the reincarnation cycle as the soul reunites with 'all that is'.

We each drop into the reincarnation cycle at different points on the wheel. Some of us started our journey a long time ago and are old souls with a depth of wisdom behind us that has been earned through the experiences of many lives. These lives have been lived in a myriad of ways, perhaps many similar lives, where we may have had a vast array of opportunities to make choices and live out consequences and, hence, come to understand the nuances' and subtleties of intention and choice and their consequences. In this way, we are given the opportunity to deepen our experience of life and to understand our inner motivations.

We all join this cycle at some point. We come into our first life with what can be perceived to be innocence or ignorance as a new soul, fresh to the cycle of life. At this point, we have little or no experience on which to draw. Eventually, through the act of living, we become seasoned as older souls, as our experiences grow through many incarnations. Living our choices and their consequences over many lives becomes a treasure chest of knowledge that eventually mellows into wisdom, as we progress on our soul journeys. Old-soul wisdom is earned over many lives, often with blood, sweat and tears, as well as joys and thrills, showing what an adventure of discovery we agree to, in coming into life.

Of course, there is no need for judgement around new or older souls, just as there is no need for judgement around youth and old age. They simply 'are'. We just have to be aware that a new soul cannot know what they don't know or what they have not yet experienced. Whereas old souls have much deeply etched knowledge in the fabric of their beings through countless repetitions. Indeed, one of the lessons that more mature souls may need to be aware of, is that it is not helpful to newer souls to try to prevent them from having painful experiences. It is likely that the advice will not be listened to or taken seriously, because the person concerned owes it to themselves and this life, to experience and learn for themselves through the act of living. This includes the consequences of the actions they take, just as old souls have done. The soul journey itself is the adventure.

Of course, we try to protect children as much as possible, but as they grow, we know that good parents have to loosen their reigns and trust that their children will find their way, at their own pace and time. By doing this, parents show faith in the spiritual journey that we are all on, even though we may be at different points on the same road. It is experience that creates wisdom, over time. As parents or older souls, we need to cultivate the wisdom to only offer advice if it's sought. Otherwise stand by and let others go with freedom to create their lives as they wish, just as we do. That's what we're here for. We all start this long spiritual journey as new souls at some point, with each life being a new page on our soul journey, providing us with the perfect landscape for creation and potential growth.

Desire (Kama) is the driving force of life. It is what brought you here, yet again. It is the desire for experiences and adventures of all kinds, such as sensual pleasures, involving taste, sound, smell, touch and sexuality. We require thrills of all kinds, including the desire to continually push at the boundaries of what is possible and what we can manifest in co-creation in the physical realm. Hence, some of us are driven to climb mountains, sail the oceans or go to the moon. We desire love and relationships and, in essence, we are all looking for completion and searching for what we lost on our entry into the cycle of life as we were plunged from the 'oneness of all that is', into illusion. We pursue our desires for money, knowledge, skills, fun and comfort as we gradually begin to remember our spiritual core and our potential to receive and give love. It takes a while to realise that this is what is driving us forward to express and experience.

From a Vedic perspective, wealth creation is a vital part of that spiritual journey. Artha is wealth creation and is very much a part of our soul experience. In being able to create or manifest wealth by using our imaginations to create something bigger, better or more beautiful, we are again pushing the boundaries of what is possible. We are using our physicality in the material realm to create more, in every sense, starting with more wealth, so that we can experience more of everything.

Having no money is limiting. It means that we can't have a good education, travel or take advantage of opportunities that would otherwise allow you to grow. Wealth, for most of us, is the first base to provide us with the sustenance for life and allow us to continually expand our thoughts, intentions, knowledge and skills into more possibilities. Nature and 'all that is' is in agreement with you realising your abundance and your ability to create whatever you want. It is in agreement with you to create and constantly recreate. That's what the universe and life force is constantly doing; prolific creation and re-creation.

Creating wealth becomes a tangible theme that can help us to grow our faith and skills in ourselves as creators, so that we can go further to create, not only big bank accounts, but also experiences that fill us with joy. In creating wealth, we have to utilise a wide range of skills and attitudes to overcome fears, anxieties and limitations, so much so that this becomes a vital personal development experience in itself. We need to dare, not only to dream, but also to utilise courage and focus, to create our realities, with our growing creative powers.

It is natural to desire, achieve and enjoy, and then once this is accomplished, desire more and achieve more to enjoy. This is in congruence with nature and with universal energy because it is also continually expanding and recreating. We are part of that cycle and, if we are to achieve our potential as human beings, we need to embrace our abundant desires as part of our spirituality.

However, here is a word of caution. This is a time of excessive consumerism, freely available credit for many people and a society conditioned by the marketing media into believing that we should be able to have whatever we want and have it now, with no need to plan or save. Hence, there are many maxed-out credit cards, broken relationships, bankruptcies and repossessions of homes, cars and other goods. This happens to people who wanted a nice life but were not able to afford it or did not have the knowledge, skills or necessary commitment to generate the wealth they wanted or to fulfill their desires in a sustainable way.

I remember someone, who I will call Janet here, who was married with a 10-year-old daughter. She harboured a huge resentment towards her husband, who earned a small income, had no interest in expanding his career and was relatively content with little. This was a problem because Janet, in particular, wanted to be wealthy and chose to try to make money through investing in the stock market, while insisting that their daughter attend a private school. The family had nice cars and goods, mainly on credit, and I met her at a time when her life appeared to be falling apart. She was very upset by the fact that the family had gone backwards financially during a stock market boom period because she always seemed to be buying and selling at the wrong time and they were now in real danger of losing their home. She refused to find a job whereby she could contribute to the household budget, so that they might eventually bring their finances into a healthier position. Janet had a belief that her husband should be able to do that on his own, because she saw her role primarily as a homemaker. She had a dream of running a business of her own and felt that she would be selling herself short if she settled for a more mundane job as an employee to alleviate the looming crisis.

There are many problems in this story, which will be discussed later.

Mature souls, through their experience and knowledge, have discovered their ability to create. They know how to put their intentions and thoughts into action by creating their reality in a tangible manner. They also know (perhaps from previous lives lived in scarcity and limitation) that, in order to live a free and enjoyable life in this physical environment, material abundance is necessary and part of their entitlement as creators. If comfort, travel, exploration and expansion are to be experienced with joy, then freedom from financial stress must be present. This means that your financial base must be sound. If your financial base is not sound, then the first task is to make it so. This requires imagination, courage, perseverance and action, for most of us. For some people, wealth and good fortune appears to simply fall into their laps without effort. I will discuss this later. However, most of us need to be able to walk before we can run. Of course, we need to be able to create an intention and dream and then take one step at a time towards its realisation.

One view of how creation takes place is demonstrated in the following text.

Neutral matter or formless matter, as Wattles referred to it, permeates everything. It is fertile potential for creativity. All it needs is the impulse of intention of any kind. Neutral matter is imprinted into creating form through thoughts. This can take place through short or long periods of time, if it successfully imprints.

If, let's say, after reading this book, you start to actively create wealth in a conscious way and this is a new pattern for you, I don't know how long it will take for neutral creative matter to receive a suitable or solid enough imprint, for it to materialise into reality. If the imprint is well focussed and clear, it may take place relatively quickly, but, if the focus is interspersed with doubt or fear or a basic feeling of unworthiness, these are also involved in the imprint on neutral matter. Such neutral matter will have a confused imprint and will, therefore, reflect a confused reality. It is likely that a successful positive creation won't take place until clarity and self-esteem are significantly improved. In this way, a clean and clear imprint may be made on neutral matter. This delivers what is required to manifest into reality with ease and solidity.

Considering the people in *The Secret*, perhaps they are more advanced souls. Maybe they have the knowledge and inner resources already formed from previous incarnations, so are poised and ready to be brought into reality. A reality that forms with ease by using the intention with deep intention and clarity, that has the creative capacity for abundant materialisation into the present. Some of us have the capacity to create clarity and consistency in their intention while others don't seem to have to put so much effort into their intention. Perhaps this is why even with a positive intention, some have to work hard to make it happen.

If we consider that the creative impulse in neutral matter is neutral, as it has no preference for how it is imprinted, it can be imprinted by ANY intention, positive or negative. Look at the chaos of the world that we have all created en masse. We have provided imprints in neutral matter that are a mixture of confusing messages that have the effect of making chaotic realities, combined with more positive messages. Any clear positive intention is rendered impotent in the final outcome of such a mixed imprint. For example, if I really want to be rich, but I don't know if I can do it, or sustain it, or have a fear that someone will steal it from me, I am giving out a series of mixed messages. What can neutral energy do with this? It has no preference; it simply imprints the messages, just like a computer, can only do what we instruct it to. It too has no preference. The preference is ours to imprint and direct.

I believe that old souls have an inner knowing about the awful reality of starvation and poverty and have overcome their fears and traumas, but retained the essence of this knowledge and learned how to create reliable financial structures from the available resources within and around them over countless lives. Having learned how to survive, they have learned that there are many ways in which they can work to create wealth and that this may be an enjoyable process. Its creation is an enjoyable life experience. Such older souls know that time is their life and is precious and not to be wasted. They know the importance of survival as paramount to everything else. Know that they must provide for themselves and their families if they are to not only survive but thrive, so what they do with their time is important.

If you are connected with your natural abilities and desires and have developed necessary skills and knowledge, and are in tune with your life purpose and committed to success, then so it will be. This is a clear and consistent message to imprint on neutral energy. Life purpose is closely attuned to passion and driven by desire and motivation. Such creation is enjoyable. For such people, work does not feel like a burden, rather it feels like a creative activity. Living within and through your life purpose is one of the most rewarding things you can do with your life. Life purpose is the basis of passion. If you live in your passion, you are doing what your soul desires you to do with your time. Time is your life.

If you expect wealth creation and spirituality to happen without passion, intention, vision, commitment and action, then it may not materialise unless you have a heavy destiny of wealth coming your way, as discussed.

When we look at the four main elements of life purpose, we are all born into (Dharma, Artha, Kama, Moksha), those of us with a strong sense of Dharma are very aware of right action, even above wealth creation. Dharma, from the Vedic perspective, is a quality of 'right action'. A quality that is concerned with 'doing the right thing'. This involves being responsible and sensitive to those around us, such as pursuing goals while keeping in mind our social or ethical commitments to others and the environment. The point I am making here is that we each come into life with a life purpose that may be Dharma-driven, Kama (desire) driven, Artha (wealth) driven or Moksha (spiritual) driven, above all else. However, those who are more driven by spirituality alone, are at the more advanced stage of their reincarnation cycle and have already mastered wealth creation, which is one of the earlier tasks of the younger soul. This means that wealth creation, as a development task, has already been accomplished in an old soul. They know how to make sure they have enough and is a prerequisite to the stage they have reached. They may have enough or plenty, but this is not their primary concern, so they can focus on their spiritual life.

It is important to reflect on what your main purpose is, because it could be that money in itself is not your primary driver, other than creating enough to follow your particular life goals. However, being able to survive and even thrive, is an essential first step in developing your ability to create and understand your true nature as part of the creative universe, so it is important in itself and very much a part of your spiritual path.

There are many people who make money, at any cost, with little or no ethics. Who are driven by a strong desire for wealth. This is the level of their soul development and many of us may have been at this stage at some point in our soul journey. So, perhaps we need to refrain from judging them too harshly. For many people, wealth has become a life purpose in itself, in an attempt to fill a deep hunger for something that they feel will complete them. They may do anything for the mighty dollar. They may have no thought about the environment or the poverty caused to others by their actions. They don't concern themselves with the fact that they already have so much, that more will actually make little material difference and bring them little joy. They are on a quest to win or acquire as much as they can, no matter what. It has become an obsession.

I believe that for many of us witnessing this kind of single-minded, ruthless attitude displayed by the actions of some individuals, world financial institutions and corporate bodies, only serves to repel many gentler, fair-minded and compassionate people from joining the ranks of the wealthy. So much so that many people are consciously or unconsciously persuaded to stay away from wealth, other than acquiring enough for basic needs.

Wealth creation and spirituality involve feeling good about what you do and also how you do it, and taking responsibility for the effect you have on others. If what you do is for the betterment of everyone, as far as you know, then it is in full accord with Dharmic law while also fulfilling your desire for wealth and adventure and is very much a part of your spiritual path.

This means that you need to give some thought to what your intensions are and also what effects your creations will have on others. How you invest or spend your wealth may all need to be considered. For example, you could invest in coal seam gas, the fossil fuel industries or nuclear technology or, alternatively, in micro-investing, sustainable land management, forest regrowth or renewable fuel technology, just to mention a few possibilities. Any of these could probably give a good return on your investment, but your heart may feel more at peace with some choices than others. So, you may need to listen to your heart if you are going to feel good about creating and maintaining your wealth in being rich and spiritual.

Of course, having wealth means that you have more resources and are able to manage the material part of your life with more ease. This leaves you more time and clarity to decide how you would like to use your creative energy. You have more power to influence the world around you and create the kind of world you would like to live in. How you use that power is indicative of how spiritual you are.

Being at the Moksha stage of your journey is to become liberated or awakened, so you can leave the wheel of life. This can be shown in the Vedic chart of those who have reached this stage of soul development, which is normally a tiny percentage of the population at any one time. Many people who have reached this level of spiritual development are not actively focussed on money because they most often have all that they want and need and are capable of creating their reality easily, because this was an integral part of their growth as wise old soul.

We are all involved in Artha (wealth), Dharma (right action), Kama (desire) and Moksha (liberation) at some level, with each of us having more of a focus on one or more of these areas than others, according to the experience our soul has reached. Desires and, hence, our specific life purpose are underpinned by the impulse of Artha, Dharma, Kama and Moksha. In a Vedic chart, it is relatively easy to identify life purpose. For some people, this is clear and they are often clearly aware of their calling from a young age. Many people have combined life purpose, though often with a common theme that changes or develops over their lifespan. While others may find their purpose to be less clear. In other cases, those without a clearly defined life purpose normally find it harder to commit to any one path and perhaps this confusion is their path, what they are meant to experience. To float more freely and find out if having no focus gives them the happiness or love that they desire at their core. Each soul is ultimately searching for happiness and expects to find that happiness in the pursuit and achievement of their purpose.

Each life is born with a purpose, because life is seeded from desire. Each soul chooses what it wishes to experience in each life. A purpose that is heavy with an innate desire to experience, master and enjoy. But, ultimately, our purpose is to discover our oneness with 'all that is'. To rediscover ourselves as creators and to reconnect with love.

Anyone reading this book has the chance to become wealthy if they are prepared to follow the guidelines. However, it is a choice to act on them, or not.

Remember:

- We are connected to all things.
- We are small within the scheme of 'All That Is' and simultaneously great too.
- We are creators.

Take time to reflect and answer the following questions:

- What is the theme of your desires?
- What do you most enjoy doing?
- What is your life purpose?

If you are in tune with your purpose, you will be fully engaged with what you are doing and being. For those who are not yet clear, reflecting on the questions above may help you to find more clarity. This is a necessary first step to becoming rich and spiritual. Your life purpose can be shown by an examination of your Vedic chart with a Vedic astrologer, or you may simply reflect on what lights you up, what you enjoy and what excites you.

Once you understand your drive and your reason for being here, it is easier to be clearer about what you want to experience at each stage of your life. Your life purpose may allow you to experience different elements of living at different stages of life, or there may be one strong theme throughout. All are equally valid.

When you come back to your goal, do you feel anticipation and excitement or do you feel heavy?

Is your goal in keeping with your life purpose?

Behind passion is life purpose.

Chapter 9

The Cosmic Map

As a Vedic astrologer, I am constantly amazed by the accuracy of this spiritual science to show character, life purpose, career, finance, relationships, fertility and spirituality. For those people who do not believe in astrology or are sceptical, I don't know if it's possible to persuade you if you hold strong views.

I started life as a physics and chemistry teacher and appreciate methodologies that work in a measurable, replicable and observable way. However, while science and rational thinking are important to me and a vital part of modern living, they do not provide the answers to the bigger questions of life, or provide meaning. Human beings require more than facts, figures and statistics to achieve harmony and contentment, because we are embodied spirits. We are not machines. We are so much more. Human beings are meaning-making, conscious beings.

Humankind is always looking for answers to questions, such as:

- What happens after death?
- How do we come into being?
- Why are we here?
- Is there a purpose to life?
- Is there only one life or are we in a cycle of reincarnation?
- Is there a God or creator? And many more...

To attempt to answer such questions, we may have to go into areas of knowledge and experience outside of rational thinking, perhaps into art, music and creativity of all kinds. Including metaphysics, philosophy, spirituality and faith. It is likely that such questions may never be answered by science. Perhaps this is why the mystical and esoteric, philosophical and artistic aspects of human consciousness continue to thrive. So that we can intuit, imagine and connect with the other faculties of our humanity, in our need for understanding and expression of who we are, rather than remaining in the confines and limitations of the purely rational mind.

When looking at how astrology could work, it is necessary to have a view that we are very much a part of nature and the cosmos. If we consider that the tides are formed from the gravitational pull of the moon on the Earth's bodies of water and that the human body is composed of at least 70% water, then perhaps we can begin to appreciate some of our bigger connections. How we are influenced and influence. If this is the case, and if we consider that we are composed of the same stardust as the moon, bodies of water and the planets in the cosmos, why shouldn't it be possible, or even likely, that we may be integrally linked to the cosmic forces? Be influenced by the energies of planets, such as gravity and other factors, transiting the Earth? Just because this has not yet been scientifically explored or proven, probably because most research is driven by financial interests with a particular goal (profit) in mind, it doesn't necessarily mean that astrology and, in particular, Vedic astrology, are invalid.

We perhaps should remember that there was a long period of time when the Earth was thought to be flat and those who had proof that it was round were vilified until the spherical nature of the planet could no longer be denied. This is the same as 'climate change' continuing to be denied presently, in particular by those with the most to gain from continuing to pillage the planet for profit, regardless of the consequences. Knowledge, reality and truth are notions that are constantly changing. They are not absolute; rather, they are objective. So, there is a need to be constantly seeking a higher truth and for this to evolve as our consciousness grows.

Vedic astrology is an accurate form of astrology that is still being used extensively in India by all levels of society and is becoming very popular in America and other Western countries for personal and spiritual development. It is used for practical, philosophical and spiritual guidance. Vedic astrology is sidereal, fixed-star astrology that shows the position of the planets with the same precision and accuracy of an astronomer's telescope today. It can locate the position of planets in the Earth's orbit accurately. It provides an accurate snapshot (chart) from which much information can be gleaned by a skilled Vedic astrologer, such as life purpose, personality, psychology, career, success, relationships, challenges and so on. The chart can be analysed and guidance given. It shows the karma that is due to unfold and also the challenges and gifts to be experienced. Options and choices can be explored with a competent astrologer. In addition, there is a system of planetary periods (dashas) that are used to show the timing, quality and focus of each area of life to be experienced. These are the areas where change and growth may take place and options (choices) discussed. Transits of planets, as well as many harmonic (divisional) charts are used for specific areas of life, such as relationships or career paths, so that consultations can guide the soul's journey into making the most of life by understanding the subtleties and nuances of each area and period of life and highlighting the choices available.

Western astrology uses the 'tropical moving-star system' to draw up its charts because it is based on the movement of the equinoxes. The Western tropical position is now approximately 24 degrees away from the Vedic fixed-star position. This system is continuing to move away from the fixed (accurate) position of the stars. This means that charts drawn up in the two systems vary by nearly 24 degrees at present and this gap is growing larger annually. I believe that the tropical moving-star system of drawing up charts is a system that may easily be dismissed as inaccurate, due to this discrepancy (of not casting actual astronomic positions of planets).

Particularly by those with a more scientific or rational mind. I believe that Western tropical astrology does have credibility in its own right and it remains the cousin of Vedic astrology. However, I have to admit to some bias here, as I am a Vedic astrologer.

I have been drawn to Vedic astrology as part of my life purpose and continue to be in awe of how accurately it reflects each person's life path. As there are many books on Western astrology and fewer on Vedic astrology in the West, I will leave the tropical astrologers to argue their own case if they wish.

In my practice, I repeatedly find that people who are doctors, teachers, managers or business people, or those who are finding it hard to find a career path, are clearly shown in their charts. Usually I know nothing of the person I am to have an astrology consultation with, other than their name and birth details. I have come to trust that those whose charts indicate that they are highly educated and possibly doctors or CEO's, always turn out to be so, as are nurses or teachers or, alternatively, those who are struggling in life. In addition, major changes in life are always shown astrologically, as are relationships and pregnancies and many other aspects of living. So, I believe that this is a very appropriate avenue for those who want to find or confirm their life purpose through looking at many areas of life and at wealth creation, which is the focus of this book.

All that is required to create a chart is a date, time and place of birth. I am always amazed at how individuals are already doing what the chart indicates they would be doing for that period of life. The chart shows the karma that is to unfold at specific points in earthly time. From a Vedic astrology and philosophy perspective, these are all karmic conditions and situations that either have already come to pass or are due to unfold.

Karma is a word that many fear and is largely misunderstood. Karma means action. Many of us in the West see it as predestiny or fate, which totally opposes the notion of free will and personal power, that we feel we are entitled to. Entitled through our conditioning through our culture, personal development and the popular psychology of our time. Conditioned into a belief that free will and personal power are the holy grail or entitlement of modern men and women. Part of the philosophy on which *The Secret* and *The Law of Magnetic Attraction* and much personal development industry is based. Free will being the key prerequisite, suggesting that we each have the ability to manifest what we want in our lives totally. This is a major source of misunderstanding, misinformation and ignorance.

From the Vedic perspective, we are each here to experience life through Dharma (right action), Artha (wealth creation), and Kama (desire), in order to awaken and reconnect to our 'oneness' and creativity towards Moksha (liberation), so that we can break free of the reincarnation cycle and move into other realms. This forms a spiritual journey through many lives that is all-engaging, irresistible and exciting and, until we are ready, we have no wish to break free of it.

What a study of karma and astrology teaches us is that the successful people of the world are not necessarily following a set of simple steps to create what they want by simply using the Law of Attraction in one lifetime. There is a lot more to it than that. They are living their karma, following their life and soul paths. Those who have a clarity and compulsion in what they do, comes from soul experiences of former lives. It's not an accident or simply luck that they are successful. They may be following the steps of *The Secret,* but they are also clear about their life purpose, passion and have all the knowledge they require to put it into action. They have set themselves up probably over many previous lives to come into fruition now. This is why a young person can appear to rise into great fame and fortune with apparently little effort, while the rest of us have to work consistently for moderate success in the middle or later stages of life, or may not achieve it at all.

The Cosmic Map

Following life purpose is a vital element of success. Someone who is gifted as an artist could not simply follow the Law of Attraction by attempting to become, let's say, a banker or a scientist, unless they also have those natural inclinations. To be successful, you need to be fully connected to your life purpose and live your passion, or alternatively have a strong destiny. Having a strong destiny means that you have already done all the work or prework required for this gift of success to come to you in the present. Trying to transfer your passion to an area of knowledge or skill that has the potential to make money, but is not your life purpose or passion, is not likely to give you the wealth and satisfaction you want. However, it may sustain you while you remain open to other possibilities and may be a necessary part of your journey. Many people do one thing while they create another. This is fine and, in fact, shows determination. To be successful, you need to be aware of and in tune with your life purpose and be creative with it in the adventure of life.

I don't want to dampen anyone's spirit here, so don't become despondent. The fact that you are drawn to this book and this topic is a strong indication that you could very well be absolutely ready to become rich and spiritual.

How in tune do you feel with your life force? Give it a rating between 0-10, with 10 being the highest.

Can you see the connection between life force, passion (desire) and your goal?

We are all connected.

Chapter 10

Richness of the Spirit

Spirituality is a richness of the spirit. This involves emotional fullness and an acceptance of yourself as you are, which leads to an acceptance of others as they are too. We are all born with the full spectrum of human qualities, from the highest to the lowest, and can choose what we engage with and how we want to be. We are no better or worse than anyone else, although we are each responsible for ourselves and our effect on others, to some extent. However, it is your life, so you have a 100% responsibility for making the most of it and may steer it in any direction you wish. Having a rich spirit will enable you to give and receive love, and be strong, generous and also humble with others, while having faith in a universal energy.

For the purpose of this book, I am presenting my view of spirituality with a broad brush and I invite you to form your own view. Essentially, I believe this experience of life is the road to awakening your spiritual nature. Life is your spiritual journey and spirituality is the journey that is life itself. You are an embodied spirit in human form and an integral part of the flow of life within the animal kingdom. Spirituality is not separate to the act of living. It is as much a part of the journey as is dealing with your bodily needs, such as going to the bathroom, the acquisition, consumption and enjoyment of food, sex and the appreciation of objects of comfort and beauty. It also includes how you deal with what you perceive to be ugly or disgusting because this is all part of life. Everyone is on a spiritual journey, whether we are aware of it or not. We are each at a particular point in the cycle of life on the spiritual journey, without exception. This may also extend to animals, plants and the environment itself, by being part of a unified sea of creative energy and life. We are part of the animal kingdom and that of the cosmos.

Richness of the Spirit

We are a part of everything within the planet and the universe. This has been and continues to be verified by the latest in scientific theory where we notice our connections with each other and our environment, even in very subtle ways, ranging from the minuscule to the gigantic. For example, it is now possible to measure the effect that a ripple from the flutter of a wing in one part of the world has on something else on the other side of the globe. This action is not lost, no matter how small. It is part of the whole. It has an effect. We are all connected on the planet and beyond, and very much a part of a consciousness far beyond our human awareness. We are part of universal energy. The creative forces at large culminate in the creation of humanity, which many people like to consider to be the pinnacle of creation so far. Such is our collective ego. Each human being is made of the same substance as other living things; we are the same and yet we are unique, much like each of the stars in the night sky.

We are physical in a material world and we are energetic too; physical and energetic beings simultaneously. The physical is easy to see, feel and validate scientifically, while the energetic components may, for the most part, only be intuited or felt in other more subtle ways. However, the importance of energy is only just beginning to be explored through the latest in physics research, such as the quantum, string and chaos theories. Until recently, the energetic aspects of being human in a physical world, where energy is a fundamental underlying presence, have largely been ignored or discounted. There are many ordinary folk with a deep connection with themselves and their environments that have somehow felt an awareness or inner knowing, faith or intuition about the presence and importance of energy in their daily lives. Energy permeates all things and also the spaces in between, and its primary importance is now being validated by the latest findings in branches of physics.

It seems that energy came first with the 'big bang' exploding into light, sound and, eventually, coalescing into particles. The particles formed the planet that made up all aspects of physicality, such as soil, air, water and eventually, living cells. Everything was motivated by the energy of a life force that drove the cycles of fundamental elements into the formation of a planet, spinning on its axis and creating cycles within cycles through its movements through day, night and the seasons. This is the same force that drives the life cycles of the stars and the galaxies. Energy is continually being transposed from one form to another and into millions of creative manifestations constantly. One of which is the physical form. Physicality has form and is composed of and supported by energy that may appear to us to be illusive, due to the limitations of the human sensory systems of vision, touch and hearing. Wonderful though it is, the brain is limited in human form by not being equipped to understand or recognise all that there is around or within us. This is evident by what we know of the different frequency ranges of animals compared to ourselves, such as the sharper hearing range of dogs. This should remind us that, just because we can't hear or see, due to a note or colour being outside our range of perception, does not necessarily mean that those energetic frequencies do not exist. There are likely to be vast ranges of realities outside our human range of perception in our world or in the universe.

Imagine energy all around you, within you and throughout the solar system and the universe. Neutral energy that has no preference or bias, in that it doesn't need to be used for good or evil or anything in between. It just is. Now imagine the latest evolved creation of living form, humankind, with consciousness and the power of thought, reflection and desire, set free in this physical plane to play, discover and utilise the elements it finds itself in, initially for survival. Eventually, as humankind begins to notice the power of thought, it finds that it can somehow influence its own reality and what it desires through its mind. It begins to notice that when thoughts are fearful and anxiety-ridden, this is what is created and terrible things happen. Conversely, when thoughts are optimistic, adventurous and respectful of itself and it has clear intentions, interestingly, good things happen. It's as if the thoughts have power to engage or utilise form into the spaces within and around it and to influence those who are in agreement with these thought forms coming into being. This same principle operates for both positive (enjoyable) through to average and more negative (painful) manifestations alike.

Spirituality is about how you perceive yourself in the world and how you co-create with creative forces; how you perceive yourself with nature, relationships and how you make meaning of life. It is demonstrated in how you treat the people in your life, from the car park attendant to the CEO of a company.

Spiritual awakening can happen in many ways and can take place through a formal religion of some sort, where you seek and find guidance on how to be a good person in the community and forge a relationship with your image of God. All religions provide a pathway to an image of God, whatever name you give to omnipresence. The problem is when one religion, as most do, takes that next step in claiming that their way is the ONLY way. Ego, arrogance, defensiveness, competition and conflict arise and a separation from 'oneness' occurs. This becomes an 'us' and 'them' mentality, which is the exact opposite of the omnipresence of creation and would probably be in opposition to the beliefs of the great founders of the world religions, such as Buddha, Jesus, Muhammad, Moses and the Vedic Rishis, to name only a few.

I believe that, with the breakdown of many religious orders and a general mass rejection of being told how to think, feel and act in the world, due to the evolution of humankind towards free thinking, there is a movement to embrace freedom of thought in many communities, showing that we are in a new paradigm. On one side, there does appear to be a rise in law and order issues and criminality, but there is also a rise in a deep and meaningful search for what moves and also enriches us.

However, as I have said before, we are all essentially on the same journey, just at different points along the road. Some people are at earlier stages of the journey, where they haven't yet realised their spiritual centre or their ability to co-create with 'All That Is'.

We all start at the same point. Some people are at later stages along the road and are gradually awakening to some of the deeper facets of themselves and their desires and motivations, while others still are already old souls. Old souls can be recognised by their wisdom, regardless of their education or physical age, and their mellowness, humility and compassion. Old souls don't often talk about right and wrong, good and bad, because they know that these all have a place, that all possibilities reside in each of us, and that we are all equal at our core. There is no need for distinctions that separate or put others up or down. We are all searching for love and ultimate fulfillment, and need to find it for ourselves in our own ways. An old soul will somehow know that we are all connected as 'one,' so to be critical, judgemental or cruel is pointless because this involves being so to oneself as well as to another. As I am you and you are me, we are reflecting ourselves in each other. Old souls have compassion and love for themselves, which is why they are so with others. You will see and feel it when you meet such people.

We are all embodied souls in a physical human form; energetic beings locked in our intestinal and vascular systems, where the sap of life flows in combination with the breath of living, uniting our bodily functions with the natural environment. We are a human form that cannot exist without the air and nutrients that the planet provides and therefore, we need to remain grounded and rooted in physicality. We are also spiritual beings embodied in a material plane that is on a journey to reconnect to a 'oneness,' that we only have a hint or vague remembrance of. A bit like a dream; a remembrance, that is reaffirmed on our return to our spiritual centre at the end of each life. Then we return to the womb of creation to rest and reflect, before being drawn out again by the allure of our God-given desire, back to Earth, on the wheel of life.

While here on Earth, we become entangled with the elements around us. We master survival and begin to master our ability to create from vision, intention and thought. These are the thoughts that shape our universal energy into reality. Thoughts are energetic vibrations that, when clear and focussed, can manifest into objects and situations. Creation has no preference for how it is formed. It is formless; pure potential. All you have to do is to imprint on it; shape and solidify it with the imprint of your visions, thoughts, passions and desires.

Look at the world. Look at its perfection and the chaos that we have created as humankind through our thought forms and actions. Look at your life and ponder what part you may have played in its creation through your thought forms. The world is a mirror of our chaotic thoughts in physical flow. There is no judgement here. It is a perfect playing field for mortal souls to explore and fine-tune their abilities to manifest, each of us doing so at different points on our spiritual journey by utilising nature's prolific fertility and abundance to create. A profusion of beauty, wonder and inspiration, as well as chaos, cruelty and also an abuse of power and resources. We have been provided with a perfect place in which we can experience all things and especially the results of our creativity, so that we can discover ourselves and hone in on our skills as cocreators. We have all chosen to be here at this time; to be part of this mass consciousness. Even though we have no memory of it.

Creating wealth is a vital part of our spiritual journey. We are free to create our thoughts, wishes, joys, fears and anxieties. We are already doing so. The planet is a perfect place to experiment with desire, intention and manifestation in the search for reconnection with the love and 'oneness' that we all crave at our core.

This forms the blind desire, within our illusionary (Maya) state, to have experiences of every dimension. All experiences are valid on the spiritual journey because we each need to find out what is worthwhile and what connects us to love, or not. We all have to go through depravity, at some stage, to help us realise that this does not stop the nagging feeling of emptiness. Bank robbers, rapists and murderers are all following a need to fulfil their desires and emptiness. They think or hope that their actions will give them something of value or a gratification of some kind. Perhaps we have been there too, in present or in former lives, and this is why we know that this way is not for us this time around. How else are we to learn? Of course we have to experience the consequences of our thoughts and actions, to feel peace, happiness, sadness, guilt and shame. How else can we learn what is worthwhile and joyful? We are meant to experience it all.

Being spiritually evolved involves being connected to our heart centre, which is the seat of our emotions and the gateway to our soul. This means that by manifesting riches, how we feel about how, why and what we have created, is paramount to our potential for abundance and spiritual wellbeing. There needs to be an alignment with our spiritual core and heart centre. Put simply, if you feel good about what, where, and how you are creating your wealth, and how you use it, then your soul will be happy. Your spiritual centre can glow. You ARE Rich AND Spiritual.

Thought forms continually formulate what I will call 'neutral energy' into neutral matter. We can think of this as a purely invisible substance that permeates all matter throughout the cosmos. It is the stuff from which we are all formed, as is our planet. Everything in it and beyond. As we know, creation is evolving, as nature continues to demonstrate, with new species and microbes constantly coming into existence, while other forms become extinct. It is evident when we look at the history of evolution and the colonisation of the planet with teeming life, that the life force is prolific. We are a part of the life force and of neutral matter that is embodied in a physical form, much like other animal forms. However, we have a mind and a consciousness that has the ability to think and create. Thoughts have power and potency, and imprint neutral energy and matter within and around us with their frequency. In this way, thoughts become the seeds of reality, so we all need to be aware of what we are thinking. Make sure that your thoughts are what you want to create.

If your thoughts are in a turbulent cycle of chaos, fear, anxiety, sadness and happiness, then you shouldn't be too surprised if you create turbulence and chaos within and around you.

If you leave your land fallow and do not weed out what you don't want to grow there, when you eventually look around, you shouldn't be too surprised to find a wild mixture of plants of all kinds (including weeds) have taken root. It may take a while to pull out the weeds so that your prized plants can flourish. It is the same with the mind. It can be full of wonderful and not-so-comfortable feelings and thoughts that need to be raked, sorted and sifted through.

This is what makes the spiritual path a challenge. Who knows why we are here or how we come to be here? I don't pretend to know, because I am like you. However, according to the spiritual teachings of Christianity, Judaism, Buddhism, Islam and many more, we are all equal. We are equal souls living in human form; we are pure, equal, portions of divinity. If we imagine that our souls are pure at their source and that we are equal, meaning that no one is of greater value than another, how is it that we are each seemingly so different?

If we take the view of being on a cycle of reincarnation, coming into life for the first time at many different points of linear time. So that some of us are older and others are newer souls, we may begin to build a picture that we can understand. If we then see that the purpose of this experience of many lives, is to come out of the illusion of our separation with 'All That Is' and awaken to our spiritual nature by consciously reconnecting to it, then perhaps we begin to find some answers. This is the teaching of the Vedas. These are the most ancient religious texts that define truth for Hindus. They came into form between 1200-200 BCE and were introduced to India by the Aryans. Hindus believe that the texts were received by scholars directly from God and passed on to the next generations by word of mouth.

During our struggles over many lives to survive, procreate and master our environment and to live with others, we form many unhealthy beliefs, suffer much anxiety and fear and create many difficult situations for ourselves. These things mask the central core of a soul, which is, simply, pure love, a universal love. The soul is masked or figuratively muddied by false beliefs and distressed emotions. From the Vedic perspective, our purpose is to sift out all of the unhealthy beliefs and feelings until we return to purity and pure love that is enriched with pearls of wisdom. This is when we find happiness. We finally discover ourselves and we enjoy our richness and spirituality.

We need to let go of unhealthy beliefs to become rich and spiritual. But what is an unhealthy belief, I hear you ask? It is one that causes anxiety, fear, depression, sadness, anger and so on. A healthy belief causes happiness and love, and does no harm. So, yes, the purpose of life is to be happy and abundant, and we all do deserve this. But, in order to fully experience this, we need to refine all of our thoughts and feelings before we can go back to that state in a conscious manner on Earth. We need to awaken from our Maya (illusion). This means that we need to rediscover our connection to 'all that is' and let go of any unhappy beliefs and turbulent emotions to head towards our awakening.

Regardless of which story we have of ourselves, whether it be 'the prince and princess myth' that many of us imagine is what our life 'should' be, to provide us with a predictably rewarding and pleasurable experience, or the yogic philosophy, or the 'new view' I proposed, life is about the growth of the soul and how we go about it.

Whether you believe in one or multiple lives, each of us can and deserves to be rich and spiritual. The journey of growth on our spiritual journey has value and is not simply about the prize of enlightenment; it is also about enjoying the journey itself. And there is so much to enjoy along the way. Your life is about your journey, moment by moment. Your thoughts and feelings come from you, because you are the driver of your beliefs, intentions and emotions, and it is you who can decide to stay as you are, or change.

By choosing to embark on change or refine your thoughts and emotional state, you will find that, as clarity and wellbeing are restored, you are able to imprint neutral matter with a clearer, more positive imprint of your visions.

Winning an Olympic medal requires many qualities, such as vision, intention, passion, structure, patience, discipline and action. To achieve the medal, aren't you also developing all of the positive attributes that become the basis for anything else you may want to do with your life after your athletic career is over?

Why would manifesting richness and spirituality be any less arduous?

The good news is that it is possible for each one of us to become rich and spiritual, just as we may each work towards a gold medal, if we so choose. However, there is only one winner of a gold medal in each event. In terms of spirituality and wealth, the odds are better; perhaps we can all win in our own way, because no two dreams are the same.

Thoughts have power and form physical reality. If your thoughts are confused or poorly formed or you have turbulent emotions, the reality formed will be just like that and so will the people and situations you draw into your life.

How much do you embrace your life.

How well does your goal fit with your thoughts and feelings?

Love is the root of spiritual richness.

Chapter 11

Creation, Destiny and Free Will

When looking at wealth creation, it is likely that your Vedic chart will show an interest in being rich by having at least one to several planets in Artha (wealth) houses. If this is the case and you are doing all that you can to manifest wealth, why is it so difficult for many people to achieve?

How does it all work?

I will give you my interpretation. The chart is an accurate symbolic imprint of the psychology of the soul involved on its spiritual journey through many lives. The cosmic map (chart), with each planet placed through the houses and signs is said, from a Vedic perspective, 'to shine a light on the life' by showing the patterns of expectations or beliefs that involve what is to be experienced. These beliefs and expectations are shown in the symbology of the planets through the houses and signs in the chart, and emanate from the deepest recesses of the mind or soul in confluence with the cosmos to create reality. From my experience, I understand the chart to be the imprint of beliefs, expectations, emotional state and self-esteem that we each come into life with. These imprints may be considered, from a Vedic perspective, to be karma. If these are beliefs or expectations that each soul has, then, if our thoughts create our reality, it is clear to see how this cosmic map appears to predict or follow each person's life so closely.

Thoughts and expectations create reality, so the unconscious matter of each of us being made up of stardust (as discussed in my book, *Stardust on the Spiritual Path, 2014*) comes into existence as we come into being at a specific moment in cosmic time. We come into being over the place of our birth and are given a specific rising sign and cosmic map (chart) as an imprint of our forthcoming life. We have created these imprints freely by how we make meaning of the events and our experiences up to this point on our soul journey. The important thing to understand here is that they are OUR imprints and we can change them whenever we want, just as we can make new meaning and create new beliefs and expectations at any time. We have created them up to this point and we can recreate them now.

If we consider the possibility that neutral matter permeates everything and is imprinted by the energy of thought, then creation is a simple process. I believe this to be true overall, but the theories espoused by the Law of Attraction and *The Secret* say little or nothing about the possible time frame involved in this process. These theories appear to assume that manifestation takes place within one life, rather than from one to several lives, as proposed by the Vedic theory when looking at karmic law.

From a Vedic perspective, creation is a continuous process that permeates everything and is not limited to a single life because it is a soul journey. You are energetic and whatever energy you create has momentum. It is formed and flows out from you and must eventually return to you because you are its maker. This means that all of your thoughts, words or actions create form and come back to you at some point, either in the present or another life. Consider the familiar saying: 'what goes around comes around'. Surely it can be no other way. Whatever you have created, you must experience. It is your expectation or belief, so it must come into being.

Neutral matter has no preference because it is imprinted by whatever comes its way, just as seeds create roots wherever they can. Neutral matter has no discernment or selection for itself. Fortunately, as you begin to realise your potential power, your consciousness increasingly develops discernment so that it can begin the process of clearing your mind of unwanted or confusing messages. In this way, you can seed your intentions clearly and consciously into form with neutral matter, as you come to truly know yourself. Here I am talking about beliefs and intentions and, of course, emotions must also be involved in the mix.

We can consider emotions in two basic categories, healthy or unhealthy, with the former being free-flowing and the latter being stuck or frozen, or holding traumatised states. So, we need to be aware that emotions that are distressed, traumatic and tumultuous are also imprinting our reality. Emotions are important and a vital part of our humanity that connect us deeply to our soul, and they are there to inform us. In truth, we all go through difficult and traumatic, as well as joyful and happy times. Our emotions inform us as to how we are. They let us know what state we are in and how we are coping with life. In reality, emotions are what make life worth living.

On the other hand, distressed or tumultuous emotions, that we can refer to as unprocessed feelings, are letting us know that all is not well and that we have feelings that need to be resolved or released, so that we can relax into newer, healthier ones. If this is done well, they may settle, release or transform to healthy emotions that can help to form the foundations of healthier beliefs. Healthier beliefs and free-flowing emotions are the bedfellows of a richness of the heart and the core of authentic spirituality. Once tumultuous emotions are cleared, healthier emotions are free to inform us generally about what is good or not so good for us. The alternative is to stay stuck. If we choose to free up our emotional state, we can feel it all. We can feel happy, sad, angry or anything else, according to our experience. There are no good or bad healthy emotions, because they are simply the messages telling us how we are. Feeling angry or sad are legitimate feelings. If these are healthy, the difficult feelings may be felt, perhaps responded to and then let go of relatively quickly, in most cases, having done their role of informing us how we are.

Many people who hear the word karma may feel fear as, particularly in the West, this is perceived as being steeped in primitive superstition. There is often a misinformed belief that those who believe in karma are disempowered and have no choice, and cannot, or do not take full responsibility for themselves, because they are locked in the grip of destiny. There is a lot of misunderstanding about karma.

There are at least three strengths of karma that we all create and live. Karma is simply action that can be thoughts, words or behaviour, with actions having the greatest potency. The karma created must come back to us. All of our thoughts, words and actions come back to us. We are all souls of humanity, connected to the living world and the energetic forces of the cosmos. Our individual souls create and then receive what we have created in this or other lives. It is thought that the time frame of karma coming to fruition is dependent upon the quality and strength of the karma involved, and is part of the mystery of our unique overall karmic map.

Vedic astrology presents a graphical and symbolic karmic (belief) map that indicates what is to be experienced. All of us experience three basic types of karma that are woven throughout all aspects of life. The first is fixed karma. This is strong karma that can be positive, neutral or negative. This karma may have been built over time from many events, or possibly from a single strong event, and is set to come into fruition in this life, no matter what. Karma, in itself, can range from the most positive and pleasurable experience to the opposite, with everything in between. When considering *The Secret* and the successful people shown in there, it is very likely that they are experiencing fixed, positive karma that provides them with an elevation into fame and wealth, easily. Of course, fixed karma can be positive or negative. It may also show itself in a sudden downturn of fortune that may appear to be inexplicable, but somehow could not be avoided. This is fixed karma. In the case of the downturn in fortune, all that can be done is to find the best way to deal with it, or live with it. Being angry or vengeful about it can only create more of the same, as all thoughts, words or actions form karma (action). Therefore, we need to be aware of our responses to situations.

If you look at your life and notice what themes appear to have a movement of their own and cannot be averted, you may be looking at fixed karma. The family we are born into falls into this category because it cannot be changed, whether it is favourable or not, as is your body type. For some people, health is fixed karma, whether it is positive or negative. For example, having good health regardless of poor lifestyle choices, is fixed karma, as is being born with poor health from birth, in spite of the best efforts to live healthy. In reality, we all have some fixed karma as well as other kinds of karma.

The second kind of karma is mixed, mid-strength karma, which is not as strong as fixed karma, because it can be changed with consistent effort and persistence. All of us have this kind of karma. It may also be greatly assisted by personal development, prayers, meditation or therapeutic processes. The key is that you must be persistent and sincere in your intentions to want to change it. All karma can be positive (pleasurable) and ranges through to the very negative (unpleasant). It is simply action. We create it, even though we may have no conscious memory of its creation, particularly if it has its roots in a former life. On a psychological level, problematic mixed karma is often to be found in the unconscious mind or generational patterns that sabotage our more conscious wishes or goals, as discussed in Chapter 4.

The third type of karma is light karma. This is the karma that gives us the most power to make changes now, if we so choose. With this karma, you can easily see your wishes or actions coming into reality, and often quickly. It is this karma that is often assumed by people involved in personal development and wealth creation, while often being ignorant of the other kinds of karma (thought patterns), that may be present.

Light karma is what the Law of Attraction is assuming, for the most part, is present. However, many people in the modern West, either do not know about or acknowledge karmic law and its differing strengths and complexities. This is vital information that explains why some of us create wealth so easily and others struggle. We all have a mixture of all three types of karma and, if you are interested in developing wealth in your life, it is likely that you have a chart that is ready for the next stage of growth to master wealth creation. So, if what you are doing is not producing wealth, you may need to look at your actions and be prepared to examine your beliefs, intentions and emotional states, and also your sense of worthiness. Through this, you can make adjustments until you start to see positive results. Many people give up along the way, because it often requires time, vigilance and persistence.

Have you ever wondered how it is that several people in a particular career or industry, in the same location, with the same education, resources and experience, achieve different levels of success? One of them may be highly successful, while the others struggle. Perhaps the answer is that, even though they are all living in this time and place, they are most likely on different points of their spiritual journey and have different levels of awakening, awareness, clarity and focus. They have accrued their own specific karmas, beliefs and expectations. Perhaps some of them have a strong destiny (expectation) for success, while others have a range of more mixed or light karma (beliefs) in the areas of career, business or wealth, which means they need to work either less hard or harder to get positive results.

As I have said before, karma is not punishment. Karma is not delivered from an external source or a vengeful God. If we consider that we are all part of creative energy and it is part of us, then we are co-creators and create by our own thoughts and actions. If we create our own reality, this means that when things are tough, it's most likely because we've made them so. There is no one else to blame. At some level, we have created this situation and so we must experience it. How we deal with what we have created is vitally important, because this will create more of the same. Therefore, responding with blame, anger or violence must result in this coming back to us at some stage, in this or another life. It can have nowhere else to go except back to us, its creator.

However, on another level, tough times often do have a silver lining. Many people report that the most difficult periods of their lives were times of transformation and they can often appreciate in retrospect that the crises were necessary to initiate changes in their attitudes or actions. There was a shift in consciousness that formed a change in reality. There are also many people, perhaps the majority of us, who consider such periods of misfortune to be unfair and do not, or cannot conceive of any possible silver lining in the situation, and are also not prepared to reflect in this way. They see themselves as a victim with life happening to them and their image of God, not doing his or her part to save them from suffering. Rather than seeing that they are in fact the initiators of their experiences. Feeling unfairly treated or like a victim takes away our power. Hence, in these cases, where there is no change in attitude or perception and, therefore, no learning, so the psychological pattern has no choice but to continue. In this way, people stay in patterns until they finally become so frustrated with the repetition over many lives, that they eventually become motivated to find a way out of it. They start by experimenting with their responses and start the journey of looking inward to how they are contributing to the situation and make the appropriate inner changes.

Reflect on your life and choices and what you have not been able to change and where you have been able to use free will. Does your goal fit with your free will and destiny?

Creation, destiny and free will are One.

Chapter 12

Taking Control

Dealing with Mixed-Strength Karma. Here is a simple example from my life. I was away visiting my daughter in England recently when my computer hard drive died and, on returning to Australia, the first thing I had to do was buy a new computer, set it up and restore backups that I had fortuitously taken, and reload software. I also needed to communicate by internet about various upcoming events, meetings and personal development seminars in my business after my extended lack of communication, due to my absence.

Once my computer was operational again, I found that, for some inexplicable reason, I couldn't enter many of my essential operation sites, such as my website hosts and domain storage sites and my newsletter site where my extensive newsletter list was stored, because my user names and passwords were suddenly not working on many different accounts.

On the same day, two days after arriving home, I found that my landline phone was not working either. Communication had suddenly become a major problem because most of the accounts that needed to be sorted out were overseas and I couldn't be in contact to sort it out without a functioning phone. At that time, I was also in the process of having a book published and having a website developed, and therefore in the middle of many negotiations that required extensive overseas communication.

My phone company diverted my landline to my mobile number saying that I would have to pay the costs of incoming calls going to my mobile phone. In my eagerness to renew a viable phone contact, I agreed to this, not realising that I could have refused, because it was the phone line that was at fault, so I should not have to pay the costs of a diversion. Within the next 30 minutes, I received four international calls diverted to my mobile phone; two from England, one from the USA and one from India. It was hard to believe.

Four days later, on Saturday morning, when it wasn't possible to make any of those essential business calls to sort out the entry into my various accounts, as it was outside business hours, I received a call from the phone company to let me that my landline had been fixed. However, by Monday morning, my phone was not working again and had to be diverted to my mobile once again. When the telephone company eventually came to see me several days later, it was found that there was a problem with my phone handset this time. I had to find my receipt and get my phone exchanged at my local electrical shop. In the meantime, my credit card machine stopped working. The provider changed it a week later and, when it still didn't work, told me that they had to change it from a sim-card version to a telephone-linked device. This meant that I had to have an electrician put in an extra phone point so I could have a working credit card machine. Three weeks later, my credit card device was working again.

Obtaining access to new software downloads to replace those on my former computer and accessing other essential accounts was much more problematic. I had moved house six months earlier and set up everything for my new address and phone number without too many problems but, for some inexplicable reason, this time I was encountering many problems proving who I was. Interestingly, this was not a problem at all when I had moved six months earlier. Since the move, I had a new email, phone number and postal address and I was finding it very difficult to prove who I was in the increasingly high security IT environment. There were many hours, days and weeks of frustration with emails going back and forth, and international phone calls and, more than three weeks later, everything gradually became operational again. During this period, I also developed sciatica (back pain) and had to have acupuncture treatment.

How Did I Deal With This?

I simply had to be efficient and persistent, and remain calm for each interaction and visualise everything working again very soon. I also chose to be very diplomatic and polite in my phone calls and emails, because I wanted the people I was dealing with in the various call centres to assist me, and I knew that it would be all too easy for them to ignore a faceless, angry customer on the other side of the world. I regularly meditated and expressed my gratitude for all of the things that were good in my life, such as my overall good health, children and grandchildren, my recent safe trip, my house and many other things. To sort out the problems, I set myself lists of people and organisations to contact systematically each day until each issue was resolved.

I did become frustrated and exhausted, but I knew that being angry would not have helped and, in fact, would have made it significantly worse. At some level, this was happening to me and it was mine. It was my karma. At some level, I was responsible for it, even though I had no memory of causing it. I was experiencing medium-strength, mixed karma. Fortunately it was not fixed karma because it was resolved after a lot of persistent effort. I had to believe that it would be solved, and it was. If it had turned out to be fixed karma, I probably would have lost my business and had to start again. At one stage, I thought that this was going to be the case and then, in one day, more than three weeks after the start of it, everything was resolved. Medium-strength, mixed karma can be resolved through persistence and the development of a good attitude.

The Unfolding of Cosmic Time

In Vedic astrology, the chart is a snapshot of the planets over the place and time of your birth. In this system, there is also a planetary-period system that flows from birth throughout life. Each person experiences the karma that is due to flow to them according to the quality and placement of the planets in their chart and the planetary period being experienced at that time in their life. For example, during this period of major communication and technological issues I was in a very troublesome planetary period or dasha.

The karma was triggered to come into fruition at this time.

So, from a 'new view' perspective, what had happened? At some level, deep in my unconscious mind, I had an imprint or expectation or fear of something that created a cut in communication and a threat to the function of my business. Even though I was not aware of this, or why, this is what I had created.

This challenged my beliefs, patience and ability to be diplomatic, and my problem solving skills and persistence. If I really wanted this to work, I had to sort it out. What I did, I believe, was the best I could do under the circumstances, by simply getting through each part of it until normality was restored. Of course, I need to create an easier belief that daily living is not problematic and, for the most part, it's not, but at some level, hints of those old beliefs must still be present. I must have created the chaos that I experienced at that time.

Who else could I blame?

What is the point of astrology if it is all about beliefs and expectations and we are creating them anyway? It gives us a bigger picture of our soul journey.

Each planet in your chart will have its time to come into prominence and to provide experiences of all kinds. Looking at your chart with an experienced and compassionate astrologer can alert you to deeper psychological imprints and emotional states. Can show your hidden beliefs and, hence, expectations, as well as your view of the world in all aspects of life. By doing this, you can have your awareness raised and start the process of transformation. This is a useful tool.

Fixed karma may also be thought of as destiny (heavy belief) or fate. Sometimes difficult fixed karma is necessary to force us to make the inner changes that are necessary for the next step in our evolution. We must experience what we've created.

Transformation, at the deepest level, often takes place through the most difficult times. These are often the events where we let go of old patterns or structures and take on something new.

While many people have a strong destiny for fame or fortune, meaning they have already done the preparation for it previously, likewise, others have a strong destiny for infamy, imprisonment or falls from grace, that cannot be avoided. Each soul has its own theme.

If everything you do in life 'turns to gold', so to speak, it is likely that you have some fixed, positive karma and, if the opposite is true, you may be dealing with mixed or fixed, difficult karma. This can also be considered to be destiny. In dealing with destiny or karma, you must not forget, whether it is pleasurable or painful, that how you deal with it and those around you, is crucial in creating more karma. In fact, how you respond to good or bad luck, is highly revealing of your true character.

Being forced to change your attitude or actions, if done in an attitude of sincere, positive intention, must have an effect on your feeling and thinking. Making deep inner changes that will surely transform your karmic imprint (belief or expectation). The way you deal with and perceive situations from that point onwards must also change. This may or may not be able to change the outcome of a crisis, but it will surely change your karmic imprint for the future.

In more recent years, the brain has been found to have a 'plasticity'. This means that the brain is not hardwired, as was previously assumed, and that new neural links can be formed and old ones can lose their strength over time, as our changes become deeper repeated in forming a new pattern. This is very good news for those of us who are wanting to improve ourselves and, in particular, to change our beliefs around wealth creation, to name only one.

Most of us are born with mixed karma (medium-heavy belief), in terms of wealth creation. Hence, there are patterns in and patterns that may need to be changed to smooth the way for success. In these cases, simply visioning and doing affirmations may not be enough to overcome them. You may have to figuratively 'jump through hoops' and hone your skills, acquire knowledge and make a consistent effort to overcome restrictions. Perhaps you have to learn discipline and develop persistence, or learn to be more comfortable and grounded in your approach to making money. Alternatively, maybe you need to become clearer about your life purpose or develop a vision, passion or the courage to pursue your dreams. There are many possibilities here to consider that I will go into later. You will only find out through your experience of life, what is true for you.

Light karma (light belief and action) is where we have the most control in directing our life. It can be considered to be free-will, because it produces easy and tangible effects that can manifest into positive or negative results relatively quickly.

Successful people are most likely to be older souls, or souls with very positive, fixed karma, with a strong destiny for success. They are living out the results of a good attitude and actions in life, probably from many previous lives. Interestingly, some of them may have been born into poverty and difficult circumstances in this life, but have nevertheless created a vision and had the determination to excel in overcoming their restrictions. They are an inspiration to us all, because they show that anyone can overcome adversity or a poor start in life. In fact, a poor start may be the ultimate hidden gift, because it puts us under the most pressure, so as to push us to harness and develop our creativity, in the struggle to get us out of difficult situations. Misfortune may be the trigger we need to wake us up and provide the momentum for change, growth and transformation.

Timing is interesting. While we may feel that we are ready for what we are creating, in reality, it may transpire quickly or take a while. In some instances, perhaps we also have to acquire patience and faith too. The reality is that there is time for everything in our lives. Time for joy, happiness and success, and time for loss, grief, sadness and anger too. They all have a place in the map of life.

There is a time for focussing on relationships, career or adventures and there is a time for creating desires, as well as a time to realise them. To be realised in this or the next life. (I am speaking of time here as linear, involving a past, present and future, even though there are many different ways of perceiving the nature of time.)

When using our creative power, we need to be aware that not all that we wish for may be granted. Perhaps something better will come our way in a different form, or perhaps what we desire is inappropriate for now, or our intention is not so clearly formed. The exercise of persistence in itself is transformative by encouraging clarity and focus, which are great attributes for life to create wealth.

Free Will

When considering free will, I wonder if it is possible that there is more than one theme going on.

Firstly, there is our karma or psychological imprint on neutral matter. This is what we have created and what we expect and, therefore, what we form according to our thoughts, words and actions. Perhaps, there is also another theme that is not simply coming from a deep psychic imprint or karma as we know it, but coming from a deep agreement of our soul with the greater soul of 'All That Is', saying to our human form something like,

"So Yildiz, you think you are pretty cool when everything is going your way, but how will you cope with this?"

In such 'soul agreements', perhaps we are provided with situations that will push us into really tight spots and force us to dig deep to find our hidden resources and creative potential, as part of our journey towards growth. In this, way we are forced to face our biggest fears and demons, as we find ourselves under extreme stress or trauma. Our inner structures and resistance to change may be forced to disintegrate as we surrender to discover our true nature. Our resistance crumbles as we find an easier simpler truth in how to 'be'. Either way, whether it is through karma or a 'soul agreement', we create our reality in cooperation with the greater workings of universal energy.

The important point here is that you always have free will. However, while there is free will of the soul, there also exists the wilfulness of the ego and personality, which often is in opposition and feels that it knows better. So, often this conflict is an internal one, until a point of surrender is reached and connection and peace is restored, if the choice is made to allow this to happen. Your karma is yours; you create it freely even though you may not remember doing so. By living your life, you are constantly making choices at all times. Through this exploration of karma and its consequences, you obviously have an easier time with your light karma and, in a sense, that may feel the most gratifying or disturbing, because you create and experience it quickly. With light karma, you can quickly rejoice or make amends and hence, change its imprint on neutral matter relatively quickly. You can easily witness the consequences of your actions in terms of cause and effect.

However, in terms of tougher, mixed-strength or fixed karma, you also have free will, primarily in how you respond to it. You can develop skills, determination, acceptance and resilience, and perhaps that is part of what you need to change or develop. Of course, you can also change your perspective on a situation by looking for the gold nugget, in terms of the lesson to be taken from the situation. If you choose to look inward, rather than blaming others for what is happening, you can begin to look at your attitudes, beliefs and actions, and make some very deep inner changes of consciousness. Even if the situation is slow to change or does not appear to change at all, if you have made an inner transformation, change has taken place anyway. As I have mentioned before, responding with anger, resentment or blame can only create more of the same, so it is not helpful.

You always have the freedom to change beliefs that do not benefit you and the choice of your emotional response. I know that some of you may find this hard to believe because reactions can appear to be hard-wired and out of your control. With conscious persistence and inner observation you can notice your thoughts and language, and gradually start to change them and so your reality will also respond.

By looking at free will, it is interesting to see that each soul is involved in an area of life that the chart suggests would be their focus at this time. Some might ask, where is the free will in that? What is free about following what our soul wants us to experience, which was decided before we came into this life? Each soul is universal. It takes us on the spiritual journey from life to life, Makes the choices, either between lives or through the karma it created.

In addition we can also make changes whenever we want to in ourselves more consciously, in terms of our direction and, most of all, in our responses, but first we need to be aware of the messages that we are running in our minds.

How else can we know what to change? Start with observing what you are doing. You may choose to change it or not. That's an important first step.

For example, you may say something like:

'I am not happy in this relationship, but I am choosing to stay for now.'

'I would love to be rich, but I don't have the courage to pursue my dream.'

Such statements reflect our choices and also take back our personal power in owning them. However, acknowledging them is a vital first step. Once we start to acknowledge where we are, we may be able to make new statements later, when we are ready. But, in the time before we acknowledge where we are, we don't know what we are doing to ourselves and what we need to change, in order to move in a more positive direction.

The previous statements, if they are true thoughts, state a reality and also areas where change can take place. Understanding karma is empowering because it enables you to take full responsibility for yourself. It requires acceptance in taking responsibility for what has been created, and choice in how you respond. Hence, through your response, you create more karma. So, being mindful of every thought, word and action is a vital part of creating a rich and spiritual reality.

Responsibility

At some level, there will be a need to reflect and to take some responsibility for what you are experiencing because this has been attracted to you and by you.

If you are to take control of your life, you need to take full responsibility for yourself, and that includes your karma. You have created it all, whether you can remember it or not. Remember, karma is not a punishment; it is here to show us what we have created and to remind us of what we are still creating. I believe that the soul, by deciding to come back into each life, decides what is essential to experience, in order to encourage us to 'wake up' and break down old thought structures on the spiritual path. If we accept the notion of a soul travelling through many lives, in order to experience and grow, then it makes sense that for much of the karma we face, we may not remember creating it. However, the fact that it is happening to us must mean that it is ours. The time frame of karma (belief) coming into reality may often extend beyond one life and can begin to explain why even, with great effort, what we create may take longer than we might expect to materialise, or it may materialise in a way that we could not have imagined. The process is mysterious.

We cannot understand it all, but by taking full responsibility for ourselves, we are empowered to direct our lives. Whereas, when we blame others or situations, we remain a victim and powerless. We all have a choice; one brings vitality, strength and dignity, while the other brings resentfulness, weakness and victimhood.

You are a creator and you do indeed have the capacity and ability to create your life in any way you wish. You are already doing that, however largely unconsciously. By transforming beliefs and expectations you will transform your reality. There can be no other way.

> "A man is a product of his thoughts".
> Buddha (Retrieved April 2014) from Goodreads.

Becoming rich is not as simple as many wealth creation books say, because the notion of karma and the cycle of life are often not considered. With an understanding of karma, destiny and the utilisation of free will, you may indeed be rich and spiritual.

- How do you respond to chaos or unforeseen circumstances in your life?
- Do you freeze, give up, or find a way through it?
- How would you respond to unforeseen circumstances throwing you off course with your goal for a while?
- Would you take it as a message that it was not meant to be, or become even more determined to pursue it?

Take full responsibility for yourself.

Chapter 13

Worthiness

To be rich and spiritual, you now know that, for most of us, many things need to be in place, in particular, in our inner world. You need to feel a sense of worthiness.

> *"At the root of every success or failure is self-esteem. It is the official and most important headquarters or base of operations that determines what kind of experience we attract into our lives."*
> Lee Pulos from the foreword of J. Jenson (2012) Beyond the Power of the Subconscious Mind

When looking at becoming rich and spiritual, we need to consider who and what we are, before we can develop a clear idea of what we want and what we are worthy of. Worthiness may have a karmic factor that comes from of our experience of our family of origin. This is greatly influential in how loved and nurtured we feel. We are very much a part of our ancestral line and what lies there. Alternatively, our sense of worthiness, whether it is high or low, can be based on how well we have experienced the world in this life and may be simply a personal choice.

Of course, we also need to have a sense of our life's purpose or our goals, and these are directly linked to what we think we are worth. The human mind is infinitely complex. We now know that we have a conscious and an unconscious mind, where only about 7% of our awareness is conscious. Yes, mostly we are driven by unconscious drivers and patterns, even those of us who have done lots of personal development and appear to be highly aware. Your conscious ideas are readily available, such as your decision to read this book, because you are aware of your desire to become wealthy in a good way. However, if you make a note of your self-talk and what you say to others in conversation, you may become aware of another theme that is in operation and underlying your conscious intentions. These may well be positive and in line with your goals, but they may contain such things as doubt, fear and low self-worth, or a mixture of both, positive and negative. Self-talk comes out through spontaneous thoughts or phrases in daily life for you to see, if you observe yourself. These are the thoughts and feelings that, if negative, may form a counter-theme to your goal, that sabotages your progress. Such mixed or negative thoughts need to be weeded out to allow the more healthy thoughts to imprint their potency in a positive way on neutral matter.

So, here we have our conscious wishes and, on another level, our fears and doubts running in opposite directions, providing a confused imprint. This is what is being transposed into our outer world and into reality for many of us. The inner and outer worlds are sending out different messages. If this is the case, they need to be reviewed, adjusted and refigured until the vision and intention are truly congruent. Once they are all flowing in the same direction, they can create a clearer imprint on reality through vision, passion and action.

It is important to be aware that success may happen in a way that we do not expect, so there is a need to remain open and flexible to what is coming into our lives. Many of us are presented with our wish or solution but, because we have a fixed or rigid view of what we want, we often don't recognise it if it is presented in an unusual way. As you may appreciate, this is not for the faint-hearted. As with going for a gold medal, many people will give up along the way because they do not have the staying power necessary to reach the finish line. Those people who believe that this should be easy, will give up. However, this is part of the journey and I believe that it is infinitely worthwhile because, as we refine our thoughts and come out of the turbulence and fear, we become so much more settled and happy, which is a blessing in itself.

Be clear that, if it is your destiny for riches and comfort to come easily, then so it will. However, even though most of us hope for a destiny of wealth and success if, over time, you appear not to be blessed in this way, you have to rethink if you really want to be rich. You may be required to make inner shifts that can flow into practical and structural changes that are in line with your purpose if you are to live an abundant reality. You may be dealing with fixed or mixed karma.

You will need to be prepared to be highly focussed in your visualisations to allow them to come to fruition over time, if you are dealing with mixed karma.

If we look at Janet's situation from an earlier chapter, it is possible to find many problems and obstacles in her wealth creation strategy. There were several problematic assumptions or beliefs that were influenced by elements of her personality, psychology, karma, family and societal conditioning and what she'd read about the Law of Attraction.

- She was not accepting her husband as he was.
- She was not taking responsibility for her choice in marriage.
- She was not taking responsibility for her financial or lifestyle choices.
- She had financial expectations that her husband didn't share.
- She had expensive tastes that she was not prepared to change in order to fit in with her budget.
- She refused to help her financial situation by taking work that could alleviate and possibly help the financial crisis in the interim.
- She had a dream of a business that she was working on that would take time to develop, while action was required urgently in the present.

Janet decided to enter the stock market at a time when many people were making a lucrative profit, but somehow, she was never at the right place and time to do so herself. It is likely that she has some mixed or fixed karma in this area to overcome or resolve. At the same time, her relationship was in crisis and Janet was not taking responsibility for her choice of husband or addressing the issue of the mismatch of ambition and life purpose in the marriage, and refusing open communication with her husband. Further, Janet didn't want to accept reality in several areas, especially in her choice of spending and her attitude towards paid employment, while developing her business. Her belief in what she had been reading in the *Law of Attraction* was such, that she was having a hard time letting go of her dream of positive change materialising simply through visualisation. She expected her wishes to materialise without having to make the inner and outer changes that were necessary, to give her goal a healthy place to form. She was refusing to face reality even though it was patently clear that what she was doing, was not working and she was about to lose everything.

Some of these problems may, on one level, be karmic, involving mixed or possibly fixed karma. These may also be seen, on another level, as deeply embedded, unhealthy or dysfunctional beliefs and attitudes. She was refusing to accept several points of reality, that were in conflict with her belief of how it 'should' be. Acceptance of 'what is', is a first step in looking at what is available and necessary for positive change.

There are certain points of reality that cannot be avoided and must be taken into account.

In addition, if we continue to do what we've always done, then we shouldn't be too surprised if we continue to reap the same results. The crisis Janet was facing was an indication of her unsustainable beliefs and intentions, not being in alinement with the situation.

Changes, if we choose to make them, can take place in a range of time frames. However, the human psyche is such, that deep change often takes time to penetrate all of the layers of consciousness and take root in new neural pathways. Hence, change is often not instantaneous, although this may be possible for some. The initial awareness or realisation may be instant, but the deeper changes of thoughts and behaviour can take longer to come into line with the new awareness. These are pathways driven by intentions, thoughts and actions that provide healthy roots for new thoughts and, hence, new forms of growth. This could be the beginning of a new way of imprinting neutral matter if someone like Janet were to choose to reflect on her beliefs and the situation she had created, and make changes. In truth, it is hard but possible, to let go of deeply held beliefs.

In reality, you are in control of how quickly you can recognise and let go of what no longer serves you, and take on new attitudes or beliefs. You have always been in control of what you have and are creating, as well as who you are. The sooner you really 'get' this and take it in fully, the sooner you will be able to let old, unhealthy beliefs go, form new ones and create more positively in your life. However, this is not so easy to observe in yourself because you are in the centre of your perceptions, beliefs and feelings. Many of these may be subconscious and so are not within our view.

If you find yourself asking, 'but what about my terrible childhood', or 'the injustices I've had in my life', or 'my lack of education?', then you are avoiding taking responsibility for yourself. At some level, you have created what is present now. Even being born into your family, culture or socioeconomic group is part of your karma, as are the choices you have made up to this point. It's what you do with it now, that has the capacity to make a difference and change your fortune. Lamenting over what should or could have been, is staying in victim mode and ensuring that you remain helpless and stuck in old patterns. Taking responsibility is to take control of your life, while blaming or avoiding others is to remain stuck. This may seem harsh, but as soon as you take full responsibility for yourself, you become empowered. This is the key to transformation. Again, this is simple, but for many people, it is not so easy to do.

Look at the life of Nelson Mandela, a great man. He had to become great by refining himself and becoming resilient in the face of adversity. He changed his understandable anger over the injustice of 27 years of imprisonment, over his protest of the treatment of black people as second class people in their own lands, into compassion, determination and a passion for change. He refused to give up on his vision of justice for his people and he displayed patience, persistence, courage and structure to put his vision into reality, in what appeared to be an impossible situation. This is a great example of someone having very difficult, mixed-strength karma, who made the inner changes necessary to transform a position of adversity into that of inner strength, that he was able to utilise for the greater good. Who would have thought it possible that someone could go through so much suffering and come out older and mentally and emotionally so much stronger, and more resilient than before, so as to form a new future for himself and his people?

By looking at your beliefs around wealth, check that they are congruent with your life goals and aspirations.

- Look, in particular, at any beliefs around limitation, scarcity and self-worth, and consider where they came from.
- Consider if they are your own or whether they come from your family, culture or religion.
- What would change if you let them go?
- What would you put in their place?
- Play with new possibilities, until you feel comfortable with them.

Some beliefs may be easy to let go of or change, while others linger on. Even though you may have a list of very logical reasons as to why you should let them go, you may find that they remain in some form. It could be that a belief is locked down with an emotional state of anxiety, sadness, guilt, shame, trauma, or deeply held tradition. In which case, you may need to seek help to make the inner changes.

As I said before, for deeper beliefs, because they are often unconscious and you are in the centre of them, it may be impossible for you to challenge yourself. Those beliefs that are conscious are the ones that are more easily dealt with, while those that are deeper, may be in the unconscious mind and much harder to locate and change. From a karmic point of view, the conscious mind can be thought of as light karma, in that it is more visible and open to free will and choice, whereas those deeper thoughts and feelings are unconscious and are more likely to be involved in stronger, mixed-strength karma, involving deeply entrenched beliefs and conditioning that require more effort to locate and transform. The unconscious is more than 90% of your mind.

In addition to the conscious and unconscious elements of the mind, we are an integral part of our family system and culture. This is the third area of human psychic structure. This is known systemic, generational or ancestral. We have a conscious, unconscious and also a systemic mind.

A systemic pattern is one that is imprinted into our unconscious through our family system that roots in previous generations. We receive many positive attributes from our family system but the negative patterns or dynamic that repeat through generations in a family system arise from such things as secrets, injustice, trauma or exclusions that could not be resolved in previous generations. The pattern is often felt by those in the present. Such patterns can sometimes skip a generation and come out in us in the present or in our children. Through this, it is possible to be part of a trail of anxiety or fear of starvation in a family system that has experienced great hardship, or any other unhealthy pattern, so that, for example, even though you may now have a plentiful supply of food, you may still be aware of a fear of hunger.

In terms of wealth, a person in the present may experience a feeling of guilt at having 'so much', compared to their parents or grandparents or further back in the family tree, particularly if they come from a family that has experienced great poverty. This can be felt as or referred to as 'poverty consciousness'. Such a deeply entrenched feeling or pattern can be a powerful inhibitor to becoming rich unless it is resolved.

Your sense of worthiness is a major driver towards becoming rich. There is no doubt that we all hold a vision of ourselves that is formed by our sense of worth. Those with low self-worth will aim their goals accordingly, compared to those with a high self-worth. We achieve according to the vision we have of ourselves. Worthiness is a major monitor of success.

Are you worthy of your goal?

Notice what thoughts and feelings arise when you consider this.

Worthiness is a prerequisite for achievement and success

Chapter 14

Being in the World

Being in the world is necessary, because we are spiritual beings in a physical plane. Is it possible for us to have our feet planted squarely on the ground, while we expand beyond our limitations to our highest potential? Surely this is what we are here for. We need to be as real as possible. Being real is to be authentic and to have integrated our inner conflicts and dichotomies. This possibility is now very much present in mass consciousness. Particularly for those of us who have reached the stage in our spiritual journey where we know we can be so much more than what we have been up to now.

There is an upsurge of personal development in the modern world that is, ultimately, about finding peace and growth with ourselves and others. Happiness and contentment is what we all crave at our core and can be monitored in how we are, how we feel and how we interact with others and perceive the world. At this point, we are challenged to come out of fear and limitation and go into love, expansion and abundance.

To become real, we first have to be honest about where we are. How can we make the necessary changes without taking a realistic view of where we are? Look at your inner world and observe how comfortable you are with yourself. Then reflect and notice each of the following qualities in yourself and rate them on a 0-10 scale, with 0 being the lowest:

Anxiety	_____	Unhappiness	_____
Fear	_____	Pessimism	_____
Sadness	_____	Optimism	_____
Anger	_____	Happiness	_____
Excitement	_____	Trust and faith	_____

Being in the World

Taking care to be real about your feelings here is an important part of the task, because repressed feelings simply go into hiding and emerge when we are not aware and in ways that we don't intend.

Of course, feeling lucky and optimistic is obviously more conducive to positive creation, just as feeling anxious, fearful and pessimistic is conducive to creating problematic expectations and outcomes. As you know by now, you create through your projections of thoughts, feelings and intentions. If you are projecting fear, sadness or anger, then that is the vibration you are imprinting on neutral matter. And the opposite is also true. Emotions let you know how you are. They are important and inform you about what is pleasant or not for you. They may also come from difficult situations and may be learned or taken on from those around you by being part of a family system.

As mentioned before, it is necessary to be optimistic and to be able to visualise wonderful possibilities in order to create abundance. Therefore, it is necessary to become a glass-half full rather than a glass-half-empty person. If you have been a glass-half-empty person until now, you may have wondered if it is possible to change yourself to a glass-half-full person. As you are reading this book, you may already have more than a glimmer of this possible reality, otherwise you would not have continued reading. As the writer of this book and a worker in this field, I believe that it is absolutely possible and, in fact, it is each person's duty to themselves to make this transition from a glass-half-empty (if that is where you are) to a glass-half-full person, if you truly want to fulfill your potential and live abundantly. I would not be doing the work I do, if I didn't believe this is possible. There would be no point. My work with people constantly reaffirms that it is very much possible. For each of us, to change many aspects of ourselves, most especially our beliefs, expectations, thoughts and feelings about abundance. However, it does require persistence and conviction to make these changes.

The way we feel influences what we experience. A beautiful day is just that, but this is not what we see if we feel sad or angry, or have any other difficult emotion. All we can see is our sadness or anger. We can't see the intrinsic beauty of the reality. This separates us from our ability to experience joy, and shows us that we need to be able to deal with our feelings in a better way. One way of dealing with uncomfortable feelings is simply to feel them. That's right. Just let yourself feel them. To start with, you will need to single them out and decide which feeling you are going to begin with. Find a quiet space in your life and focus on the emotion by feeling it in your body, without going into the story of how it got there, because this will take you off on a tangent that will keep you stuck, which is not the purpose of this exercise. So, simply focus on the feeling for a few minutes, stay with it and then let it go. You may need to repeat this several times over the next few days or weeks, until you notice that the strength of the feeling is lessening and it will eventually disappear. If it doesn't disappear, you may choose to seek the help of someone who can assist you further with this.

If you are a glass-half-empty person, you can challenge yourself by pushing yourself to notice the simple good things in your life. Take yourself out of the mask of pessimism, look up and see what is good or pleasing in each moment. Notice really simple things, such as the colour of the sky, blades of grass, the complexity and beauty of the veins on a leaf, a nice meal, or a good cup of tea or coffee. Notice clouds or the quality of a raindrop as it touches your skin. Just start to notice all the realities in each moment. Perhaps you are not in pain and your body is comfortable. You can just acknowledge that and stay with it. As you begin to see the good things in your life, you will notice your mood changing. Gradually you will make the transition from glass-half-empty person to glass-half-full person until, eventually, you will notice that you can hardly remember a time when the glass wasn't half full for you. Once this happens, you have made a major transition.

Being in the World

You do have a choice. You can choose to see the goodness in everything around you or not. This does not mean that you need to be totally naïve or foolhardy or an extreme risk-taker. You can keep your common sense and your life experience close at hand to inform you about what is safe or not, while also appreciating the good things in your life.

If you are a person who finds that they get annoyed easily, notice what annoys you about people or situations. When you do this, you will probably find a voice in your head going on about how it 'should be', rather than how it is. Where did this voice come from? Is this a parent's voice or someone else's, or is it simply your own? If it comes from someone else, you can visualise them and give it back to them. Then come back into yourself and request a new voice to come in that gives you light, joy and freedom. If the voice does not come from anyone else and is your own belief, perhaps you can challenge it and make a new one.

By digging deeper, we will find beliefs about how we think things SHOULD be that cause us to become ruffled with indignation when people or situations do not fulfill our expectations. These are unhealthy beliefs that are rigid and lead to many disappointments, because other people and situations cannot not fulfill such rigid beliefs or expectations of how things should be. Having such beliefs leaves us feeling cheated, rejected or poorly treated. We cannot control others or situations that are outside our realm of influence and neither should we. On a personal level, the ONLY control we have is of ourselves. We are in control of the way we are and what we create, and the way we experience our reality. This is a huge task in itself, because it is the primary part of our soul's journey, so why torture ourselves with expectations that are unlikely to be met? Beliefs that are unhealthy have rigid expectations that are bound to fail us and may be considered to be unhealthy because they do not accept the world or others as they are. This results in uncomfortable emotions and disappointment. They ensure that we remain unhappy. Unhealthy beliefs are unhealthy for us. Throughout this book, it is clear that you are in charge of your reality as a creator, so why create a reality that is fraught with disappointment or limitation?

Changing such beliefs or expectations must change perspectives and the outlook on life significantly. Sounds easy, but this requires persistence and time that may benefit from some professional help, if you can't do it by yourself.

Alternatively, you may find that few things disturb you because your beliefs are flexible and help to ensure that you are happy and content generally. If you have flexible beliefs, you won't expect others or situations to live up to your view or a rigid view of the world, for the most part. If this is how you are, you will have a healthy respect for others having their own ways of thinking and acting and being on their own journeys. Your view may be open and generous, and not have overly high expectations of how others or situations should be. Healthy beliefs are in line with happiness. There is no doubt that we create our own happiness or unhappiness.

Of course, you are not in isolation, because you are part of the world and your social and family circles. Who you choose to be with or are born to also has an effect on you, and you on them too. You need to be aware that, if being with certain people brings your mood down, you can choose different people to hang out with. However, if the pessimistic people in your life happen to be family members, this can be more difficult. You can still make your own choices here by how you choose to be with them. You can choose to embrace your own growing positivity and continue to notice the things to be happy about in your life. If you do this, you can let those attitudes come through in your conversations and ways of being. People around you may notice the change and, if you persist, they will eventually get used to the new you. Alternatively, they may find the new you too confronting and withdraw by choosing to hang out with those of a similar mindset to themselves, so that they can feel comfortable in their complaining. Personal development will indeed change you and it may not always be possible to stay close to old connections as you change your mood and allow your mindset to evolve.

However, family do remain family for life, so they must be dealt with at some level if your soul is to be at peace on your quest to be rich and spiritual. Family are part of your soul karma, so they are not a mistake, and will need to be dealt with in a good way, where possible. Simply cutting them off is often not a solution, as Hellinger, the founder of Family Constellations in *Acknowledging What Is* (1999) stated, as the soul has a deep loyalty to the family we are born into that can be felt as guilt, if such a rejection is made. Rejection has consequences in the family system that may be felt for generations.

I know that many therapists and therapeutic modalities encourage people who have been deeply hurt by family members to simply cut them out of their lives. I do agree that this can be helpful to start the healing process while they become more assertive, in giving them space to heal because, but this is not the long-term solution, from a holistic or spiritual perspective. If we consider that this relationship is in our lives, it must be here for a reason and, if it is not possible to have a satisfactory connection with the person/s concerned due to violence, abuse, or mental illness, then all we can do is find a place of healing for ourselves, at some level: While acknowledging our place in the family system and the greater family soul. By acknowledging our and others parts in the relationship, we can take responsibility for our part only and leave the rest with those concerned. In this way there is no need for blame. Karmic law will take care of the rest, so we don't need to concern ourselves with retribution or the need to be right by making others wrong.

As human beings, we are individuals who are also part of a generational family system and part of 'All That Is'. By being spiritual, there is a move towards 'Oneness'. Cutting off has no place in this, although we may indeed need to create good personal boundaries around what is and what is not appropriate for us. It may indeed not always be possible to have the quality of relationships that we would prefer with some people. According to family constellations' theory, cutting off has repercussions for ourselves and our children in the family soul, because it is felt as a deep wound in the family system that has the effect of being played out repeatedly in future generations, unless we deal appropriately with our part in it, in the present. According to Hellinger, if we cut off from a parent, we shouldn't be too surprised if our children cut off from us too and repeat the pattern of pain into future generations.

As a child, all we can do is learn to see our parents as they are. As fallible human beings entangled in their own family systems, just as we are. From this place, perhaps it is possible just to connect to the love of the soul that provides us with an avenue to come into life.

As a parent, all we can do is enjoy our time as parents and learn to let our children go into their own lives and make their own choices. They may or may not appreciate what we have done for them and, at some level, we need to make peace with that.

In terms of spirituality, many aspects of how we cope with living are relevant. By looking at personal development, this can be measured by how easily and quickly we recover our equilibrium after an upset. It doesn't really matter how many personal development seminars or what therapies we do, if the reality is that we are still easily annoyed by people or situations, or can't let go of anger, sadness or resentment, then we still have a long way to go. True spirituality is demonstrated in how efficiently we are able to respond, process and let go of feelings and grudges within reasonable time frames. By hating others, are we not hating ourselves at some level too, because we are also part of 'omnipresence'?

Each of us can be happy when things are going our way, but it's how we are when this is not the case, that is more revealing about who we are.

How resilient we are in bouncing back to an easy equilibrium is what lets us know how we are really travelling. Happy people have happy thoughts and can easily attract happy, abundant situations and people into their lives. Of course, tragedy, loss and trauma happens to all of us at times, without exception, so how we deal with this, process the events and our feelings and come back to an equilibrium is key to how we are travelling and a good indication of our spiritual development. So, if you want to be rich and spiritual, make sure that you are a glass-half-full kind of person. This can require some genuine effort on your part and maybe even some professional help at times to help you make necessary shifts.

Give and Take

As human beings, we are always in a state of aloneness and connectedness. These are part of being human and involves coming to know and accept ourselves and boundaries. Many of our beliefs and negative feelings come from a confusion around boundaries in interpersonal communication. By being with others, such as friends, partners, lovers or spouses, or being a parent and family member, the art of communication and sharing is a part of the equation of being human. This involves having a healthy sense of your own place within your family system to help you to be comfortable about being you, in both intimate relationships and social situations. This sets you up to be able to fully receive abundance as a spiritual person.

The level of give and take, and the quality of the boundaries necessary, varies between people creating healthy relationships. Friendship is usually an equal relationship that respects the level of intimacy or sharing with each other in a reasonably equal manner of give and take. Generally, if the equilibrium becomes too lopsided, the friendship is likely to collapse, or if you don't receive or give what has been agreed (often unspoken) between you, it is likely to disintegrate. If you find that you are always the one who gives, it might be worthwhile looking at why that might be the case.

Consider the following:

- Perhaps it is the case that you are used to the role of giving or supporting in your family of origin?
- Or is it that you prefer to be in charge of relationships and don't trust others to behave appropriately?
- Or is it that you don't feel worthy to receive from others?

In reality, many friendships, for most of us, have a 'use by date'. As we mature, we often outgrow friendship groups unless we have enough in common to make if fruitful. Many friendships come to a point where they no longer fulfil the requirements of the original connection. Perhaps this is the sad part about personal growth. We grow our of what fitted us before.

Healthy love relationships are also about give and take. But these are more complex, intense and intimate, due to the mysterious chemistry of sexual attraction, as well as the complex symmetry of compatibility and contrast between a couple that needs to exist in order for it to work. This bond is often karmic, in that the souls have intended to meet in life in order to experience and discover each other and themselves through the interaction. All relationships form a mirror of how we are and how we are perceived. A delicate balance of give and take, symmetry, chemistry and intrigue, are all involved, as well as the search for and the giving and taking of love. Relationships involve communication and negotiation and often require letting go of the need to 'be right' and to come to a compromise. They are often our greatest challenge and reward, in terms of our search for love.

They can result in the creation of children. Becoming the conduit by which other souls come into being so that a bigger relationship group can evolve.

Being a parent is a different kind of love; a caring and protective love, where parents give and children take, in ideal circumstances. If this is the case, the child can grow up feeling loved, protected and supported, with parents providing the appropriate structure and discipline for them to explore and develop safely. This involves parents making choices that may often render them unpopular at times, in the interests of the safety and development of their child. Hence, children do not always get what they want. Parents need to feel strong and comfortable in this reality, knowing that they are working for the best interests of their child, even though this may not be appreciated by them due to their lack of development. Relationships are a crucial part of being human and a vital part of being rich and spiritual. Relationships rely on the ability to connect with other souls to find harmony, wherever possible, as spiritual beings.

Boundaries

By coming to a balance of give and take in each type of relationship and becoming self-aware, there is also a need to develop healthy boundaries. Just as good fences make good neighbours, so do good boundaries make good relationships. However, good boundaries require a strong sense of self and the knowledge of the needs or requirements of the other. An awareness and respect for yourself and of others.

What is yours or theirs and what is shared between you and how you deal with them is a delicate balance in itself. Through these interactions, we become aware of what is appropriate for each of us and how to put voice to a 'no' as well as a 'yes', when necessary. In reality, most of us, in our eagerness to be liked, loved or accepted, find it easier to say 'yes' than 'no'. The personal development required to say a clear 'no' firmly or compassionately, when necessary, is significant and requires much self-assurance and presence. Presence is required because of the risk of disapproval and the revelation of vulnerability by being true to ourselves and others. In this way, we can find the best solutions for ourselves, even though this may push at the limitations or awareness of others, at times. Being able to do this for ourselves is important, as is listening to the 'no' of others, so that we can relate well and find companionship, support, harmony and love with the souls around us. Being real with ourselves, others and our world, is vital in our quest for richness and spirituality

Take time to consider each of the following:

- Who in your life will be impacted by you achieving your goal?

- When looking at your responsibilities towards your children or partner, does your goal remain a strong and positive intention?

- If parents or society don't appreciate the value of your goal, will you pursue it anyway?

Relationships are pivotal to spirituality.

Chapter 15

Gratitude and Abundance

At first glance, the word 'acceptance' might appear to represent passivity. However, acceptance does not indicate passivity or resignation; rather it represents a combination of strength, responsibility, presence and grace. Acceptance is a natural forerunner to gratitude, grace and abundance.

If you look at nature, life force and the universe, there is a natural impulse towards growth. There is a constant natural flow towards expansion and diversity. If we look at our generation compared to those of our parents, grandparents and beyond, each generation has mostly advanced significantly in many ways. Generally, each generation builds on the progress of the former by wanting and achieving more than before. In addition, there is an agreement by parents and grandparents that their children and grandchildren are welcome to build on what they have provided, to make a bigger, brighter and better future for themselves.

If we look at the living standards of the 1800s generally, we find that conditions for most people were not remotely acceptable when compared to our modern times. Sanitation and living standards are almost unrecognisable for many of us in the West when compared to that time, even though they are still present in much of the third world now. This advancement is reflected in the extension of longevity, in general, in the West. Our expectations have expanded significantly. A much larger percentage of us in the present have degrees, double degrees or masters degrees, whereas our grandparents were often considered lucky if they had completed school up to the age of fourteen.

The point I am making here is that the world is abundant and delivers according to our expectations and our ability to receive and create. The more developed we become, the more we can visualise and create, and so the cycle of abundance continues to expand. There are no limitations, other than our own beliefs, expectations and sense of worth. It is natural to want to do well and acquire a good life style and, having done so, enjoy it so much that we want to. Then go to the next level and expand and enjoy even more. This is not greed, as some areas of society or religion may suggest. It is natural and very much part of universal abundance.

But what of the starving millions or the struggling poor, I hear many of you ask? Here is the point. You staying poor does not help them eat more or raise their living standards at all. Giving to the poor may help them eat for one more day perhaps, but does not change their lives or empower them, and often maintains the status quo between the rich and poor. The belief that staying poor helps those who are less well-off is an old pattern of belief that must be uprooted from our consciousness if we are to create positively and abundantly. This thinking comes from a view of the planet and the universe that is finite and has limitations and scarcity. This is not the case if you understand the connection of your thoughts, intentions and neutral matter that are constantly creating and reforming reality. In reality, focussing on the poor will make more poverty in the world and also create more limitations for yourself, whereas focussing on abundance will have an opposite effect. Remember, what you focus on is what you create.

By becoming rich, especially if you have come from a poor background, you become a role model for those who are struggling, by demonstrating that there is another way to live if that choice is made. They can be inspired to dream and find a way out for themselves. The best way to help others is to become the change you want to see in the world and encourage others to do likewise (if that is their wish) in their own way and in their own image.

I am not suggesting that you should be selfish. It is wise to be compassionate and helpful to others and, if you want, to help in a tangible

Gratitude and Abundance

way become part of groups that help others to become self-sufficient. Such as providing education or supporting groups where you can contribute and develop creative ways of offering real help that can become the basis of sustainability for those in need.

Join or create movements that introduce a new way of looking at the world by providing affordable personal finance. One such area of many groups is micro-investing, such as Micro Place sustainable investments (Aug., 2012. Retrieved 13 July, 2013). Micro-investing is a system where people like you or I invest. These are real investments that offer market interest rates (this is not charity), so that those who are struggling, often in third world countries, can take out a small, low interest loan. To start a small business of some sort, such as selling fruit, food or handicrafts, etc. Through this, they can gain some autonomy, personal power and self-esteem, and their children can be fed and go to school and be provided with new, long-term possibilities.

By being rich and spiritual, you will have a more meaningful effect on others if you take the time to put on your creative hat to find ways to invest and spend your money in ways that are mindful and productive, both to yourself and others, so that everyone wins. To simply give to charity without investigating the efficiency of their work is perhaps lazy (or at the least, lacking in imagination) may ease our guilt but is lazy giving. Taking the time to find out how much of what you give ends up with those its meant for, finding out how much of the money is spent of marketing, advertising or corporate salaries, can be useful information in making an informed decision of where to put your money.

Giving to known charities often absolves us from feelings of guilt about having so much while others have so little. This is a guilt that may have its roots in our religious doctrine or the poverty consciousness at the root of family and cultural systems, and humanity itself. However, it is time to consider how we can help others in new ways. I suggest that becoming wealthy yourself and encouraging others who also want this, to do so in their own way, is a great help to those in need. Providing role models or assisting in ways that help to provide the means to allow others to acquire education or the resources to become self-sufficient, is a respectful and empowering way to offer a helping hand.

Remaining poor means you that you are not in a position to help anyone and may even be a burden to others or society if you can't support yourself. Wealthy people can provide jobs for others and are consumers of services and goods that keep the economy going. Keeping money moving through the economy by wealth creation and spending on services and goods is good for everyone.

From your more fortunate place, being truly grateful has a much better effect on you and others than that of poverty and guilt. Gratitude is a better quality to foster than guilt, in terms of generating wealth and incorporating spirituality in your life. A deep 'thank you' and being truly grateful for everything that you have in your life will imprint neutral matter positively. If such gratitude is felt throughout each day and genuinely expressed, at least in your mind and heart, it can only have the powerfully positive effect of generating more of the same, both within and around you. Your gratitude may be for your home, food, health, people in your life, your business or work going well, and so on... Such constant feelings of gratitude can only generate more. They can only generate positively into neutral matter to ensure that more of the same is imprinted. This is also the case for those things that are not yet as you would like them to be: Such as a project or wish that you are creating.

The secret here is to be in gratitude for it, as if it is already here while, on another level, working on it to help it come to fruition. Take care not to make this an empty mantra by making sure that you put some feeling and vision into it to make it real, every day. Even many times each day.

This requires focus.

Make gratitude a part of your day. Say thank you for 7-10 things every morning and every night and be grateful for many aspects of your day.

Attitude

I am frequently struck by the attitudes of young people. It is so often easy to see who will create a good life for themselves and who won't, just by their presence and their attitudes to performing quite ordinary roles, such as the checkout person in a supermarket or the trolley collector, or shelf loader. Those who have a professional, efficient and respectful way of responding to customers stand out by showing an attitude to life that will hold them in good stead. Those who chew gum and make it obvious that they don't care or respect anyone, or and are far too good for such ordinary roles, also show their character. They may consider these to be lowly jobs, but for those with vision and determination, they see such roles as a good starting point to develop the skills and open up opportunities. Some people have an inner knowing that they need to develop discipline and determination to be the best they can be and become rich. They have an attitude of enjoying the journey of growth and discovery of now while holding their longer tern goals. Many wealthy people have started their lives with nothing materially and with little education, but by forming a healthy inner resolve to imagine and act towards a vision, they have created a better future to step into.

Many people interpret the philosophy of 'love your work' to be 'only do the work that you love'. Both of these ideas may be valid, but beware of giving up work or a situation that is sustaining you prior to finding a better or ideal job or position. Walking out of a job and hoping that, by chance or divine creation, you will fall into a much better one may work for a few people, but it leaves many stranded like beached whales. This can be quite a destructive move. Remember that it is your task, as part of your spiritual journey, to find ways to sustain yourself and to be able to pay for basic utilities and keep a roof over your head. This is the first step to mastering your physicality on this planet and, in so doing, mastering your financial and social worlds. We are all part of the financial reality that we have created together. So, if necessary, consider changing your perspective with respect to what you are doing now. Be mindful of what you are doing now in sustaining you and find ways to accept or even like or enjoy aspects of it, knowing that this is just a stepping stone. Do what you are doing in the best way you can with appreciation and gratitude, because this is what sustains you while you envision and create other opportunities. Consider how you can be present in your existing situation while you focus on your goal, engage in research, study or network in your own time to create your new reality. For most people, it's not wise to be reckless or impatient to cut the chords that sustain you. Putting yourself into 'free fall' with no fall-back position. However, it is true that all change is risky and risk is a necessary step to move into new realms of possibility. A calculated risk is more of a wise choice for most of us.

A good attitude and determination can take people to professional jobs or boardrooms all over the world, or into their own business, according to the vision they have of themselves. Interestingly, others who feel that certain work is below them often remain stuck for many reasons. Glass half empty attitude, lack of vision, low motivation or even a sense of entitlement driven by an inflated ego. Inflated egos are often a mask for low self-worth. An illusion of grandeur can hide the pain of low self-worth. These are states that prevent people from taking such ordinary work seriously and becoming resentful of those who move on successfully in life, on the strength of their vision and efforts.

The message here is not to give up if you are in a job that is not ideal. Do it as well as you can while imagining yourself in a new role and making the most of your current situation. If you continue in this way for as long as it takes to get a promotion, find a new job or a new opportunity, you will be actively creating a better future for yourself. For many of us, wealth creation is gained by taking one step at a time. In this way, you can gradually refine and clarify your intentions, thoughts and feelings, and gain the skills and knowledge necessary, while being open and flexible to opportunities that present themselves. All of this will change you and what you create. If you are not employed, set about changing this by working at ANYTHING, perhaps even doing voluntary work. Put forward your best attitude and do what you do with generosity and diligence, while being open to doors of opportunity opening for you in perhaps unexpected ways and places.

Unless you have a strong destiny for wealth and success coming your way, this is probably the way it will stay unless you take full responsibility for yourself and your life and become motivated to make changes in your thoughts first. For most of us, change takes place in step with our ability to grow in awareness, one step at a time, as we gradually expand and solidify our new reality. In so doing, significant change can take place over time, especially when we consider where we are now compared to last year or the year before that.

Neutral matter can't do it for you. It has no agenda. You are a creator and everything comes from you. You have to imprint it with your intention for it to know how to manifest according to your wishes. Thoughts have power, so you need to use them intentionally if you are to be rich and spiritual.

How grateful are you for what you have in your life and for life itself?

Gratitude begets even more to be grateful for.

Chapter 16

Change

So, you are ready to step into being rich and spiritual, as is your right as a creative being. You create your reality through your thoughts and actions, and now that you understand this, you can take control and steer your life towards your aspirations.

But, what if you have realised that, even though you want to be wealthier and are ready for change, there appear to be psychological blocks that stop or sabotage your progress? How do you resolve these blocks? Most of us can easily deal with surface beliefs, thoughts and feelings on our own or through talking with friends, or even through such processes as coaching, counselling or mentoring? A few sessions here may be highly beneficial to help you find clarity and more understanding of your life's purpose and passion and to help you find your motivation, so you can move on with more confidence, to live the life you want to live.

You need to be aware that for any professional or personal development process to be effective, it is necessary for you to be totally committed to the process. Your full cooperation is required. No one can MAKE you change. As a psychotherapist and mentor, it is outside my ethical framework to influence anyone to do anything that they are not in full conscious agreement with, because I am very much aware that we are each on our own journey and that some are not yet ready or willing to make those deeper changes. I am aware of respecting everyone's journey and their freedom to live how they wish, within reason. (I am thinking mainly of harm to self or others here.) For me to attempt to help someone make inner changes when they are not yet at the stage of wanting or agreeing to those changes, is overstepping my mark as a helper. Once we've had enough of our struggles, each of us starts to realise that the only person who can change our situation is us. Only at this point can anyone be ready for change.

Initially, we are likely to make external changes. This may be changes in work, education, relationships or location, and these may well provide improvement or advancement in life. However, many people may find that some of the same patterns go with them, wherever they are. These may be patterns of sabotage, fear, doubt, or lack of confidence. This can also include a pattern of perhaps finding that, wherever we go, someone picks on us. Whatever the pattern is, it appears to follow us wherever we go. At some point, we may realise that we are the common denominator in the pattern that, so it must be coming from us. Just coming to this point shows that we are taking responsibility and moving from being a victim (its being DONE to us) to an awareness where we are doing it to ourselves. We need to take responsibility for our feelings of being victimised or thoughts feelings and actions. Take ownership .This is a giant leap in growth. From this point, we can become empowered to make new choices. In short we can stay as we are, or go from being a victim to taking responsibility and taking control of our lives. This is transformation in itself.

The next step is coming to a point of readiness for the task of change and being sufficiently convinced that change must take place in order to move on, in a more productive way. Often a crisis point must be reached where the pain of continuing as you are is worse than any possible discomfort of going through the process of change. Again, each of us will reach this point at different times.

I have found that, for those who are not ready for change, it is best not to attempt to persuade or coerce them, other than to let them know that I, or others, will be there to give them support when they are ready. They need to come to this point for themselves by taking full responsibility for themselves in any area of change, in order for it to be productive, without exception. As a therapist and mentor, I always assess the readiness for change in a potential client during the therapeutic process and only proceed to assist them free their mind, pattern or behaviour if they are in full agreement that this is what they want. If this is the case, the tipping point has been reached, where it is more painful to remain as they are, than to make the changes necessary for freedom. Of course, change can take place on its own through reflection and persistence too, over time.

Steps Leading to Change:
- Reflection
- Awareness
- Taking full responsibility for yourself
- Readiness for change

Once this stage is reached, the process of change will be relatively easy.

If professional help is sought, remember that for any process to work, it should be a liaison. Each of us needs to take responsibility for ourselves and leave behind the excuses and blame and meet the therapist or coach halfway, if we hire them, and be prepared to look focus inwards to gain the necessary shifts. Unfortunately, on a practical level, many people may not reach this stage of readiness for change in this life.

Finding Help

I will outline some possible pathways to find help once you are ready and are seeking assistance. Deeper beliefs or emotions, issues or traumas can be resolved with longer-term psychotherapy (talk-therapy) or in only a few sessions with a competent, registered clinical hypnotherapist. Hypnotherapy is an effective way to locate and resolve unconscious blocks, beliefs and emotions relatively quickly for most people, once they are ready for change. However, finding someone who is properly qualified, effective, ethical and with whom you have a good rapport is essential for a good outcome. Hypnosis is relatively easy to illicit, but the skill in the therapy is what helps positive change take place, so make sure if you choose to follow this route, that you pick someone properly qualified, registered and insured.

Of course, your sense of worth is a vital issue in terms of being rich and spiritual. Where does this come from? Some of it comes with us from past lives and some comes from our family environment or our in our formative years. There is no doubt that the way we were attached to our parents in our formative years has a lasting effect on how we perceive ourselves and how we relate to others, and our sense of worthiness. How our parents were parented and then how they parent us, is full of potent messages from which we make meaning about how lovable we are. Hence, this often becomes the basis of our sense of worth. If our parents were centred, loving and calm, they may have been fully present for us in doing the best they could to provide what we needed, whereas, if they were anxious, insecure and depressed, they were likely to have been experienced as 'not present' and perhaps gave us the impression that we were not so important, special or lovable. This has a lasting impact on us, unless the perception is changed.

Many of us unconsciously absorb the qualities of our parents' attachment style with their own parents, through the qualities of the formative parent-child bond. Relationship patterns and nuances are passed down the generations and consist of a mixture of secure or insecure attachments, regardless of our parents' often-sincere wishes to provide more for us than they received themselves. Each generation is often doing the best they can with what they have, with survival itself having the highest priority.

Here we come to systemic consciousness and generational patterns, which are the patterns that we enter into at birth and are present in our very essence, mostly subconsciously. All parents generally do the best they can with what they have or know, but deep systemic and often unconscious patterns have a way of infiltrating each generation through the quality of relationship bonds, especially between parents and children. Ruppert

(2008) in *Trauma and Bonding* gives a detailed explanation and many examples of how the subtleties of relationships are transferred through generations. These patterns become the blueprint from which we operate in all spheres of life. The quality of those initial connections help us to develop our sense of self. This means that the happy, loving and attentive face of a mother has a deep impression on us, just as a cold, distracted one does, and these influence our sense of 'lovableness' and our sense of intrinsic value.

This may sound a bit grim. But the good news is that this can be changed, reformed or transformed, even if we have inherited or been born into difficult dynamics. This is particularly so when we are prepared to make the changes, perhaps with an effective therapeutic approach with a competent, well-trained facilitator. In addition, it has been discovered that the brain is plastic, meaning that it can reform or grow new neurons and is not hard-wired as was previously thought.

I am a counsellor, hypnotherapist and Family Constellation facilitator and trainer, who has found through my practice that my clients reach more rapid resolutions through processes that operate on the subliminal areas of consciousness, such as hypnosis or family constellations.

This can be done in a relatively brief therapeutic process of between one to only a few sessions, or as part of a longer process, according to individual needs, using a modality called 'family constellations' and 'business constellations'. Former therapies around attachment theory issues have traditionally been long-term and, arguably, not so effective in providing real avenues for change. In my opinion, this is due to these therapies utilising mostly long-term talk-therapy, which has a limited access to both the unconscious mind and systemic consciousness that are largely subliminal in nature and are where the roots of the problematic patterns or issues may lie.

Change

Look at the goal you formed in Chapter 3. Has it remained the same or has it changed subtly or even fundamentally up to this point? If it has changed, what are the key elements of knowledge or awareness that have contributed to the change?

No change, no gain.

Chapter 17

Family Constellations: Systemic Solutions for Success

Resolving blocks to success and improving worthiness are important steps to becoming rich and spiritual. As I have said before, your sense of worthiness is at the root of all wealth creation. How is it possible to create what you can't feel or imagine as a possibility? How can you truly step into a bigger reality unless you feel worthy of it? What you think and what you feel is what you project.

In my experience as a counsellor, clinical hypnotherapist and Family Constellation facilitator, deeper beliefs and systemic issues involving primary attachments to parents and the dynamics of the family system are more effectively dealt with using systemic family constellations or business constellations, rather than counselling methodologies. Traditionally, these take place in seminars, workshops or in private sessions. Family and business constellations involve a brief, experiential solution-focussed psychotherapeutic process that can release buried personal and systemic emotions and help individuals to find new perspectives of themselves and their system. In this way, it is possible to form new beliefs from which a person can gain more freedom, peace and a sense of intrinsic worth.

A constellation seminar or workshop consists of a group of people, who often do not know each other, meeting with a facilitator who takes it in turns to look at their issues or situations through a business constellation or Family Constellation. The group meets in a confidential circle with the facilitator and the person who is looking at an issue. They tell the facilitator what they want to look at with the group. The facilitator collects mainly factual information about the issue through a few questions of the family or business system concerned. Then the person is invited to choose several people from the group to represent those involved in the issue and place them in the middle of the circle in relationship to each other, according to their inner image or feeling of the issue or situation. In this way, the unconscious image or systemic dynamic that forma a pattern (constellation) is set up. From this point, the constellation is in progress.

Interestingly, just being set up like this creates a field of energy, probably due to the intention of the client to imprint their dynamics on the neutral energy within the group. This phenomenon of the energetic imprint is known in constellation circles as the 'knowing field'. The representatives, who normally know very little of the client's family or relationships, become aware of sensations developing in their body, such as heaviness, lightness, sadness, or anger, as they tap into the dynamics of the family. This is the energetic dynamic of the system. The facilitator allows or guides the constellation to proceed or develop with more people added if necessary, until shifts in the constellation take place. This may occur in movements between the representatives as they progress from disorder into more order, where emotions may be released and new perspectives come to light for the person concerned. The facilitator may offer 'healing sentences' to aid the healing movements of the constellation until a finishing point is reached. This provides a new perspective from which the client can make new meaning and, hence, provide a new base from which to operate.

Generally, the client will set up the constellation, including choosing a representative for themselves so that they can sit in the holding circle with the other observers to witness the unfolding process. In this way, they observe and experience the process from a different standpoint and process it through their senses and emotional body, and through the representatives of the family system. This experiential combination creates a very powerful process for change.

Family constellations and business constellations may be used to look at all relationship and wellness issues, including mental and physical health and also work or business-related issues and, in particular, issues of life purpose, intention or worthiness. Or any blocks to success.

Here I offer some example constellations to show how they may be used to resolve blocks to wealth and success.

Names and details have been changed to protect privacy. As no two people or family systems are identical. What is shared here may not be transposed to your or similar issues, as each family or business system is unique. These stories serve only as examples of how the process can unfold. If you would like to experience the process for yourself, I strongly advise you to find a Family Constellation facilitator near you who can help you to explore your own issue through a constellation process.

John and His Business

John was in his mid-30s and was frustrated about not being able to make his business profitable. Through the interview process, the facilitator found that John's father had left the family when he was nine years old, after going through bankruptcy. John grew up with his mother and had little contact with his father since then. John's father lost his father when he was a child in the Second World War.

John set up a representative for himself, who stood next to a representative of his business. The representative of the business turned and began to move away from John towards the edge of the circle, looking out, saying that he felt very tired and heavy. The representative for John looked dismayed.

John was then asked to choose representatives for his father and mother, and place them in the circle. He put the representative for himself standing by the representative mother, with that of his father in front of him. His father had his back to his son and widowed-wife.

The representative for John's mother very quickly became agitated and angry, and clenched her fists, while the representative for John said he felt helpless from being unable to help his mother.

The representative for John's father reported feeling totally cut off; not feeling anything. He was looking down and said that he didn't want to turn to look at his family.

John was then asked to put in a representative for his father's father, his grandfather. He placed his grandfather in front of his father at the edge of the circle, close to the representative for the failing business.

The representatives of the father and grandfather stood for a few minutes looking at each other, until both started to weep openly and eventually hugged and comforted each other. The representative for John's father was able to express his anger and sadness at losing his father, and was able to receive his father's regret at dying so soon.

Eventually, the representative for John's father turned to John and his ex-wife, with his father behind him. After a few minutes, the representative for his widowed-wife was able to express her anger at being left to cope on her own with their son.

The representative for John's father was able to express, through his tears, that he was truly sorry for what had happened and was eventually able to honour her for what she had done for their son in his absence. The representative for John was able to look at his father for the first time.

The representative for John's father was able to say that he felt shame for what had happened to his business and for leaving them.

The representatives for the older men held out their hands for John and, after a few moments, he moved towards them and put a hand on each man's arm, father and grandfather. The three men looked at each other with love and gratitude for a few moments.

The representative for John's business suddenly became energised and moved over to John and, eventually, John was able to stand with his business by his side and look strong with his father and grandfather behind him.

John was able to find a new perspective of himself as a man and an appreciation of how the loss of his grandfather had deeply affected his father and, hence, impacted his parent's marriage and business, and himself. John was also able to appreciate how much he had judged his father for the failure of his business and leaving the family. He was able to acknowledge for the first time how much he had missed a connection with his father. The reconnection with his father and grandfather appeared to have brought life back into the representative for his business, as he reconnected with his family system in a healthier way. It appears that John felt the loss of his father as well as a the heaviness of having to look after his mother, which was a burden for him. Further, by judging his father, he had taken on the shame and guilt of the system. With each person in the system taking responsibility for themselves in the process, it was possible for John to reconnect to the love there and look out to a brighter future.

Sandra and Her Business

Sandra was struggling with her marketing business when she came to do a constellation.

In the interview, she told of the struggle that her father's family had had with extreme poverty over many generations.

Sandra set up herself and her business with representatives. The representative for the business quickly became crouched and very tired, while Sandra's representative looked distressed. Sandra was then asked to set up her father with five generations of men behind him, using five representatives. All of the representatives for the generations of men, including the father, looked tired and weak in their places.

The representative of the fourth generation of men was asked to turn and look back at the fifth generation, bow deeply and express gratitude for what they had done to assure their survival. The man representing the fifth generation visibly stood taller with pride and love.

This was repeated by the representative of the third generation of men bowing deeply in gratitude to the fourth until the fourth stood tall with pride and this repeated in the same way down the line of representatives until the representative for Sandra was able to bow to her father with gratitude and then to all of the previous generations, and ask them all if they would all bless her to be successful in her business. She added that when she was successful, they would all enjoy it with her, in her heart.

The representatives for the generations were able to bless her and the representative for her business stood tall and said that he felt tingling sensations in his body.

Sandra took her place in the constellation with her business by her side and was moved to tears of gratitude.

Even though Sandra was a vivacious and apparently confident and intelligent businesswoman, she had felt the weight of her family's poverty on her father's side. She carried a deep, unconscious systemic loyalty to her past, as she felt the poverty consciousness of her system. This became a block or sabotage to her success. Once they were honoured for their struggle for survival, Sandra was able to accept their blessings to enjoy better times and move on with them in her heart.

In both cases, reality was accepted and new perspectives were allowed to arise.

What I have given you here is a bare framework of what happened in these two constellations that cannot possibly convey the power and profound nature of the experience of the process of family and business constellations. To observe your own situation from a circle and to become aware of other's perspectives within your system is very helpful. The process allows a release of unspoken messages and emotions in the system, and is truly powerful in offering the person concerned a new opportunity to reconnect with those concerned in a new and healthier way. From this point, new meanings, beliefs and choices can be made and a raised sense of worthiness occurs. Becoming rich and spiritual cannot take place without feeling worthy and being in a good place with the people in our life, so that we can feel good about ourselves and grow spiritually as well.

The philosophy and practice of family and business constellations may assist you in coming to a place of peace with others, even if others have not, or are choosing not to join you in that. This process has to be experienced to be understood and felt in multiple layers of perception, and is not simply role-playing or psychodrama. This is a psychotherapeutic, spiritual process that works energetically at the level of the personal and systemic (ancestral) soul. For more information and examples, please read my book, *Stardust on the Spiritual Path* (2014), or look at my Family Constellation website: https.familyconstellations.com.au.

Research in epigenetics from the National Institute of Health (retrieved 12/05/2014) joins a growing area of knowledge that shows that such factors as environmental (social, emotional, relational) and traumatic qualities can and do trigger genes on or off. These are ground-breaking findings because they show that DNA and genes are not necessarily hard-wired, as was previously thought. Just because we have a particular gene does not mean that it will become active. Social, emotional and relational factors are far more influential than biological sciences believed. This gives more validity to such processes as family constellations that assist individuals with healing problematic systemic dynamics, such as trauma or other emotional factors that hold them back. I have countless numbers of clients who have improved their wellbeing or resolved sabotage patterns to reach success through this brief, experiential process.

In the process of finding a psychotherapist to help you free up your mind of limiting thoughts, distressed feelings, or systemic issues, it is important to check the credentials of the people you choose. Make sure that they are properly qualified and registered with appropriate professional bodies so that they can assist you to make the changes you want. I believe it is important to take the time to speak with them on the phone and trust your gut reaction to guide you when choosing someone.

Meditation

Does meditation have a place in being rich and spiritual? Meditation can help you to train your mind and also connect with your family and spiritual fields. In training the mind, it is an important way of slowing down your mind, so that you can see or be aware of your thoughts, because most of us have a 'monkey mind,' until we learn to master it. By this, I am referring to the thoughts and feelings that jump around constantly and apparently uncontrollably in our minds. Meditation can help you to become aware of what is going on in your mind. Once you have an awareness of its jumping around quality you can be trained to relax and let it. In addition you can become aware of what you're thinking or saying to yourself and, therefore, what you are unconsciously imprinting on neutral matter. Then you are in a position to understand what you are creating. From this point onwards, you are in a position to know what it is that you want to change. You can begin to take responsibility for yourself and make conscious changes to create what you want in your life. There is no doubt that, to be able to focus your intentions in a positive manner, it is necessary for you to have some mastery of your mind.

On another level you can contact your higher self and the energies that connect you to your spirituality and renew and nurture yourself in that.

There are many styles of meditation available but, ultimately, meditation provides a space whereby you can meet yourself, notice your thoughts and feelings, come to a place of peace and acceptance and even love yourself as you gradually fine-tune your thoughts and process your emotions. Again, this requires a willingness and commitment to the process, as well as discipline and patience. These are all qualities that must be mastered if you are to make changes in your life and maintain focus on your intentions as you create. While there are many kinds of meditation, I do believe that there is one for everyone who wants this to be part of their life. Meditation has a gradual build-on effect that may feel slow at first, but can increase over time, as it becomes an essential part of your life.

Meditation is an essential part of my life to keep me nurtured, grounded and energised. It might not be appealing to everyone to sit in a lotus position saying OHM in perfect stillness. So, thank goodness there are many styles of mediation. This means that you can experiment with what suits you, in terms of silent meditations or visualisations, or moving meditations, such as yoga, Tai Chi and Chi Gung, or visual, guided, or any other mind/body discipline that can assist you to master your mind. For many people, activities such as walking, running, surfing, art, music or dance can serve a similar purpose of training the mind to come into synchronicity with the body and soul. By training your mind, you will have access to more clarity and focus to utilise in manifestation of thought into form.

Consider your goal with your ancestors standing behind you. Feel gratitude to the lives that have gone before you that have made it possible for you to be here.

Keep in mind that they may have no understanding of what you desire in this modern, technological world, so ask them for their good wishes in your quest.

Take your place with love and worthiness.

Chapter 18

Greatness

Are you ready for greatness? Are you willing to stand out from the crowd, test yourself in whatever field you are in and be excellent at what you do, or what you present? This does not have to be competitive. In fact, it's better if it's not when you want to be rich and spiritual. Standing up for who you are or what you can offer is simply a declaration of your contribution to the prolific abundance in the world. However, this requires confidence, courage and motivation. For those of you who are ready for this level of exposure, it requires a unique gift, skill or package of some sort that you can use. How else are you going to stand out or become rich? Being ready for greatness may take time and considerable personal development to raise your sense of worthiness (as discussed in the previous chapter), but is essential if you are to be rich. There may also be an element of risk in being willing to put yourself at the forefront. To be great, you need to be a person of influence with a deep well of knowledge or skills in your area of expertise, or have a particular talent. For most people, this often takes several years or even a lifetime to acquire, unless you are destined for fame from the start and have been born with the skills of the likes of Mozart or Rembrandt. Such geniuses appear to have talents that can be expressed even in childhood, in that they are charismatic, unique and inspiring from a young age with knowledge or skills way beyond their education, circumstance or age. Most of us grow into greatness later in life, if we are prepared to embark on such a journey.

Consider if you are ready for greatness.

- What area or areas are those to which you can aspire for recognition or success?
- Do you have the courage to go for your dream?

- Are you ready for what this may cost in time or effort?
- Do you only want success and richness if it comes easily?

Most people in the world can be put into two broad categories, in terms of living; that of 'cruiser' or 'navigator'. Cruisers form the vast majority of people and they take a laidback attitude to life and are carried in the ebb and flow of it, primarily wanting to have a quiet, relaxed and comfortable time. There are no judgements in this, as this is probably what their soul has requested for this life. Perhaps they've had a lot of storms and dramas in previous lives and simply need to cruise this time round. In addition, they may have no real desire other than comfort and ease. Perhaps living like this is rich for them, compared to former experiences.

Others, a much smaller proportion, are navigators. Navigators are the movers and shakers; the ones who make things happen. They are the leaders, visionaries and motivators; the ones who are ready and hungry for much more. Navigators often want it all and see no reason why they can't have it. They too often want to have a comfortable life and time to rest periodically to enjoy the fruits of their creations. However, navigators also have a drive that wants to push boundaries and develop, hone and fine-tune their abilities to create and continually recreate throughout their whole lives, knowing that there are no limitations. It's not simply about being rich for navigators, although this may be an initial goal, but it is also about the adventure and thrill of the creation. Creating something tangible from an idea can be an inspiring process in itself, because once you can create like this, why wouldn't you want to continue to do so, just as nature and cosmic forces do? Cocreating with creative matter, just because you can and just for the fun and joy of it, is a free and natural way to develop and express.

Many cruisers have a belief that wealth or success should come easily and they are not interested in spending their time and effort to make those inner changes required to develop their creative powers. It could be that becoming rich is not their main purpose in this life.

It may also be the case that many of us spend much of our life as cruisers and come into a very different astrological period where, even though we may not have been motivated before, we may suddenly find our focus shifts and we can suddenly become motivated to improve our financial position or our career, or have a great idea that we want to develop. We may suddenly see the need to become more independent when we find that relying on others to provide work becomes unreliable or unsatisfying. Alternatively, we may become bored with cruising and start to have a vision of ourselves doing much more. There are periods of life that are opportune to become active as a navigator and then, in other periods of life, we may feel the pull to go into a much quieter, reflective period astrologically, because this is what our soul desires for this part of our spiritual journey. From a Vedic perspective, life is generally split into four main areas. These are:

> **Student or apprentice** in life. The young person who has to make a place for themselves in society and establish a career or means to accrue financial stability to create an identity and be able to sustain themselves.
>
> **Procreative** period where the person finds a partner and perhaps creates a family and supports and guides the next generation into adulthood. A career supports the family.
>
> **Reflective** period of mature years where the person may become more spiritual by reflecting on the lessons and experiences of life as they grow into old age.
>
> Finally, if a person lives long enough, they can become a **guide, teacher and elder** in their family and society.

From a Vedic perspective, this becomes a rich and spiritually rounded life.

However, each of us are in a particular planetary period that continues to change as we travel our life path. If the period you are in involves career and finance, you will be very focussed on career and finance now. Whereas, if the period you are in highlights reflection or meditation and a need to withdraw from external activities, that is what you will be drawn to. It is said that the Grahas (planets) pull you from one desire or focus to another at different times of your life.

For example, when I was in my early 20s, I moved from a sun period, as my sun was poorly placed in the twelfth house, into a moon period. Previous to this, I had said that if I wanted children at all, it would be later in life.

Shortly after this, I moved into a moon period for ten years. The moon in my chart was sitting with Jupiter, the ruler of my fifth house (children), and was placed in my ninth house of grandchildren and higher learning. So, I experienced the desire for children and had two during this period. Then I went into a Mars period of being a homemaker for several years, as Mars in my chart was ruling the fourth house of home. Then I entered a Rahu period (north node of the moon) period for 19 years. Rahu was placed in my sixth house (work) and, at the beginning of this period, I went to university to study to be a teacher and taught for the rest of that period. At the end of this period, 19 years later, I met two astrologers in one week and became enthralled with Vedic astrology. I left teaching a short time later as I entered my Jupiter 16-year period that I am still in. Jupiter is in the ninth house of higher learning with the moon planet representing the twelfth house of spirituality and the subconscious mind. Hence, in this period, I am a Vedic astrologer, psychotherapist, hypnotherapist, Family Constellation facilitator and also an author of two spiritual books. My next period is a Saturn period, which shows a continuance of my work and the potential for this to grow.

I show my path to explain how focus can change at each stage of life. We all go through many different stages of life where what we are focussing on now is absolutely perfect for what we are meant to experience. Your chart will show exactly what you will be drawn to at different stages of your life. Hence, we may be drawn specifically to wealth in our early, middle or later years, or it may be a strong theme throughout our life. We are each unique and we also have choice in how we deal with each desire and experience as we both follow and create our path through life.

Becoming rich is very much a part of your spiritual growth. It is the way you become aware of and develop your co-creative powers. These are powers that you can use in any way you wish. However, by living in a material plane and in modern technological times, it is natural that, in the spirit of growth and abundance, you will want to enjoy as much in this physical realm and modern world as you can. This requires a plentiful amount of money to allow you the luxury and resources to continue to expand and grow through knowledge, travel and enjoyment of this beautiful planet.

Enjoyment is restricted if you have to worry about bills or rely on social services or others to provide your basic needs. How can you expand and grow when you are on the edge of poverty and in fear of annihilation due to starvation or being exposed to a harsh natural or social environment? Fear and anxiety create more fear and anxiety and so the cycle continues. What can you do about it?

Many people who are aware of the Law of Attraction and find themselves in difficult financial circumstances can still visualise themselves becoming rich, even while they are doing nothing about the practicalities of their situation. Visualising only, could work for you, if you have previously done the inner work to set the stage for wealth. Have good karma to come in soon. But, for most of us, are likely to have mixed, medium-strength karma that requires structure, discipline and persistence to change or overcome.

This requires change to occur, both internally and externally, to provide a healthy place from which wealth can take root and grow in a healthy and sustainable way.

Perhaps, for some people, going for a promotion or looking for the next opportunity is what is needed while, for others who are not yet working, it might be necessary to have the humility to take any job as a first step and be open to further opportunities of growth. Yes, it is helpful to keep a vision of what you would like and to work towards it, and to notice any fears or anxieties reduce, as you begin to make internal changes and take responsibility for yourself and what you have and are creating. Your life will change.

It is a possibility for everyone to become rich and spiritual if they are ready, or at least to improve their financial situation significantly. For most of us, it requires a lot of personal growth, awareness and change, in terms of attitude, actions and the development of a belief that we are worthy of much more. Many of us have subconscious blocks to becoming wealthy, as was explained in the previous chapters. Remember, only those who have a heavy destiny for wealth will find it comes easily to them, with little or no effort. It is likely that they have already prepared the ground in former existences.

Many of you will have tried doing little or even nothing and found that little or nothing happens. You will know if what you have been doing has worked for you or not. If it hasn't and you are ready to make the changes necessary to become rich, you can do so by maintaining and expanding a full and open heart into a spiritual experience too.

Thoughts are potent seeds that become fertile in neutral matter when they are regularly watered with focus and nurtured with clear intentions. Although this sounds easy and it is simple, such focus and clarity are qualities that need to be developed, honed and sustained. Most people can do this for a short time only and give up over longer periods of time.

Wealth is relative and is a perspective that may constantly change throughout life. We all have to start somewhere, so whether you are starting from a place of poverty or middleclass comfort, each of you has the capacity to become rich and spiritual if you take on the messages in this book. You can continually expand the vision you have of yourself and your potential for richness and become accustomed to each level of comfort and abundance, and become desirous of more. This book is written for everyone, from those who have nothing, to those who are comfortable and those who are already doing well in life. It is up to each of you to decide what level of richness you desire and are ready for.

Be aware that being rich, in itself, may not be the highest priority for many people, as relationships, health or any other area of life may take priority. So, in the area of wealth, you may be a cruiser. There may be other areas of focus that are more important for you at this point in life. If you reflect on what excites you and interests you, it is relatively easy to find out what your purpose is for now and follow it.

By daring to be great, you may not always be liked or accepted initially, especially by your peers and perhaps even by your friends or family. There may be jealousy towards you for having the courage or ambition to move into the next paradigm of experience, comfort or status. Even if you make it clear that you are not in competition with others, in the very act of daring to be noticed or to excel, you are expanding into a new image of yourself by seeking to be the best that you can be. Others may find this hard to deal with because it brings up their own insecurities and lack of worthiness or ambition. It is likely that you will lose some friends, change the quality of other friendships and find new connections. This is a big step.

We need to experiment with our will, focus and creative abilities to find out how they work. This is a great adventure of self-discovery and expansion, because the more we create and become used to how we do it, the easier it becomes. Once we can create in this sphere, we are ready to create in others, having our financial base in good order. A good financial base is necessary to provide sustenance so that we can create in other ways. This may take us to a more purely spiritual focus during later stages of our reincarnation cycle, as we head towards liberation, because wealth itself does not bring happiness. Wealth brings comfort and choice, but spirituality is a fullness of the heart and soul, and cannot be purchased. It is easy to see that many very wealthy people are not happy, particularly if their wealth has been made through cut-throat competition at any cost, using questionable ethics and abuses of power. It may not be possible for them to be content and relaxed because of their need to be vigilant and watch their backs, to fend off those who they have used or abused. They live in fear of demands for justice to account for or rectify their greedy actions.

However, being wealthy is significantly more comfortable than living in poverty, and it does bring a certain level of achievement, physical comfort and power. It also comes with a responsibility that many wealthy people do not acknowledge or honour. Bing rich and spiritual requires significant personal development to be able to walk-your-talk and become fully responsible and aware of your impact on others and the planet.

Wealth with spirituality brings comfort, riches and a power that has compassion, because of a willingness to be responsible for ourselves and our impact on everything around us, especially with those who share our life, such as partners, family, friends, colleagues, employees and our environment. This kind of wealth is that of the heart, which is the window to the soul. With this fullness and joy, it is possible to accept and even love yourself in a compassionate way, and to love all of those around you, because you know that you are just like everyone else. No better or worse off. With this kind of wealth, you can feel good about yourself.

Neutral matter is formless. It has no preference as to how it is imprinted. It is part of our initial spiritual contract that we are free to take our time to discover who we are through many lives and experiences. We are free to create the most blissful and the most hellish situations for ourselves and we do so constantly. We are always imprinting neutral matter with our thoughts, emotions and intentions, but now we can do it consciously. We do it anyway, so why not make it abundant and joyful?

- Are you ready to step into your greatness?
- What skills or areas of expertise do you have or are you going to develop to become noticed?
- Are you a navigator or a cruiser?
- If you are a cruiser, are you prepared for the effort and time required to transform yourself into becoming a navigator?
- Does the achievement of your goal require you to become greater in some capacity, or simply to be noticed?
- Notice if you are ready for this.

Dare to be great.

Chapter 19

Steps to Becoming Rich AND Spiritual

The following guidelines are a summary of the essential elements to follow for those of you who are navigators or are in the process of transforming yourself from cruiser to navigator on your journey of becoming rich and spiritual. We all have the capacity to do this at any time.

We live in an abundant universe as energetic beings connected to 'All That Is', and this involves neutral matter and the power to create. Each of you create your reality constantly and this includes the karma you have accrued from past lives. This awareness offers you the opportunity to embrace your power as a creator.

If you put together the ideas in this book and live them, there is no doubt that you will become richer. However, I know that only a small number of you will have the drive, motivation and focus to follow through and put in the effort required to train your mind to create abundantly. If you do want to follow the path to wealth and wellbeing, here are the main guidelines:

Be aware that some people want to become rich:

- through the fear of being poor;
- through the fear of failing others' expectations

These motivations often do work to help you become wealthy, but they may not result in you becoming rich and spiritual, because the latter comes from knowing that you are worthy. Knowing that you are worthy of the best comes from a compassion or even love towards yourself and others.

Coming from a place of fear of not being able to live up to the expectations of others shows that a feeling of 'not good enough' is alive and well in you. You may still become rich, but not necessarily spiritual, because self-acceptance and compassion are absent. By being rich and spiritual, you come from a place of love and worthiness.

The seven steps to becoming rich and spiritual, are:

1. Worthiness
2. Imagination
3. Intention
4. Motivation
5. Courage
6. Action
7. Gratitude

Consider your goal within each of these steps.

1. Worthiness

I have gone into great detail in the previous chapters about the value of worthiness in your life and also what you can do to improve it. Worthiness is a constantly shifting paradigm that may expand or contract according to life events. Nevertheless, it is a quality that must be present and growing when you are on the path to becoming rich and spiritual.

Worthiness is at the root of your ability to create. Without a healthy sense of worthiness, it is not possible to imagine a better present or future. You must know that you deserve this.

Assess your goal on a scale of 0-10, with 0 being the lowest:

How much do you accept yourself as you are? _____

How much do you accept others as they are? ____

How worthy do you feel? ____

Once we accept ourselves fully, warts and all, we come out of an egotistical frame of mind and into contact with our humanness that is in line with our soul. Human beings are capable of having the very highest to the very lowest qualities of humankind and, of course, it is true that we all 'stuff up' sometimes, WITHOUT EXCEPTION. If we really understand this, perhaps we can have more humility for ourselves. Stop judging ourselves so we can accept ourselves and others, just as we all are. We can relax about expecting others or ourselves be perfect, while we continue the process of purifying and clarifying ourselves on our spiritual journey. The more we do this, the more we can feel gentle towards ourselves and, hence, others.

Being non-judgemental is a commonly used term that starts with self-acceptance and worthiness.

2. Imagination

Imagination is an important part of manifestation. If you are so tied down with how things are, or have been, that you can't envisage a better present or future, then how can you create one? Imagination involves having a vision (or a feeling, for those who are not so visual) of what you are creating. Visions are thoughts made into form, often with colour, feeling and intensity. This is a vital component of co-creation and manifestation. Unless you can form a vision of how you would like things to be, your creative power remains stuck and unformed, and has nowhere to go. Creative energy will create vagueness or confusion if this is the imprint of your thought pattern, in the same way that if you set out on a journey, it is necessary to have an idea or a vision about where you are going, so that you can avoid getting lost.

Imagination is a vital step in creation because it is powerful in imprinting neutral matter into form. All thoughts are powerful in imprinting neutral matter. Scary or anxious visions are also strong so, having mastery of your mind and emotions is a necessary state to reach. If you create a fine image of what you want and then spend time in fear and doubt and imagine all the things that could go wrong, this will disturb and reform the vision into something else. Of course, you need to consider what could go wrong in an objective way as you formulate your intention and, if necessary, make choices to avert or reduce these probabilities. However, having done this, you need to go back to your image constantly and have faith that it is forming.

If your intention shifts, from a clear picture, and go back to it daily to fine-tune or change or reimagine it.

Write down the vision or draw it if you are artistic. It may be a symbol or a shape. It's anything you choose it to be. Put it somewhere to remind you of what you are creating.

3. Intention

Be clear in your intentions and make sure that they are in line with your desires and life purpose; that purpose for which you are here.

This is so important as, to end a life unfulfilled, is surely the saddest thing.

If you do what your life purpose is driving you to do, or be, or experience, then you will be fulfilled and happy. If, for some reason, you can't live your life purpose right now, then do so in your private time and especially in your visualisations. Set your intention to make your purpose the central theme of your life, while doing whatever you are doing to the best of your ability to sustain yourself and your family. Soon opportunities will open up if you remain alert and open to them, and your life will change towards your intention.

Human beings are quite capable of occupying more than one reality at one time. This is why you can be aware of being in your body while also observing yourself. You can stay in one reality, while maintaining your intention to move into another realm as soon as possible, simultaneously. In reality, this will only occur when you have imprinted neutral matter sufficiently. This means that it will begin to create form with your intention and bring people together who seek to work with you in this newly forming reality, and opportunities will open up. However it is not possible to know how long this will take. Your karma may be such that you have to prove your intention by prolonged focus to produce an overpowering imprint to overcome what was imprinted previously: For example, mixed-strength karma, or confusing negative beliefs. If your visions have been confused, don't despair, because former mixed or contrasting imprints from former thoughts or emotional patterns will fade away over time if you can maintain your present intention clearly and consistently over time. You will need to be open to the opportunities that develop, because they may or may not be exactly as you'd pictured them. Neutral matter can be playful, so don't miss what is coming your way due to it appearing in ways that you hadn't foreseen. These could be paths that can open up further doors to what may be in your best interests.

Intention is not the same as will. Be careful with the use of pure will. Will has a rigidity and narrowness about it that is not the same as intention. Intention is clear, but also open, and may take longer and have a reflective depth to it, rather than the rigid forceful quality of pure will.

An example of will is saying or insisting that a certain situation happens by next Tuesday or by the end of the year. You can't order creation. It's more subtle and profound than that, as pure will is of the ego and intention is of the mind, conscious and unconscious. So, move away from will and expand into intention.

- What is your intention? Write it down.

- How do you know when you are connected with your desires and your life purpose?

You know when you are really enjoying what you are doing or creating. Desires are the drivers for life purpose and the forerunner of intention. Without a desire or an awareness of your life purpose, no matter how small or grand, you are likely to find yourself floating aimlessly. We all have desire and life purpose because we all desire to experience the life that brought us back into life, yet again.

Reflect on what 'lights you up' and excites you to find your life purpose.

This is its essence.

For some of us, our desires are not particularly involved with wealth creation, as such. What we desire may be more about experience or expression and may be involved in an area of life that is not highly valued in society, in terms of accruing wealth. Artists of all kinds may fall into this category. Here is the challenge. If this applies to you, can you simply enjoy your artistic creativity for what it is? Or would you also like to be suitably rewarded for it? If the latter is the case, you may need to find ways of using your talents, skills or knowledge in a unique and inspirational way. You may need to go from being ordinary to extraordinary. Mediocre to great. Go from cruising to navigating. If being outgoing with your creations is not your thing, you will need to find someone who can do this for you or, alternatively, overcome your fears, find some motivation and do it yourself. Acquire the knowledge, skills and confidence to let others know about your talents.

Being in touch with your desires, passions or life purpose and having a clear intention, following and fulfilling it, will feed your soul and keep you happy. Your life will head in a more satisfying direction. Remember, the idea that 'artists don't make money' is yet another belief. Perhaps this is a belief that you are ready to replace with something more inspiring, because it is not strictly true, as many artists do make money. Are you ready to join the successful ones? Do you feel worthy enough? Perhaps you need to have more than one career before you can somehow put something more substantial together to create wealth from your passion. This applies to any profession or talent. One step at a time is fine until you can run or even fly with ease. This applies to the majority of us.

Perhaps you want to be:

- wealthy, self-sufficient or independent;
- inspirational;
- the best you can be;
- liked, accepted or loved;
- famous; or
- something else...

Consider your deepest intention and write it down.

You can then form short- to long-term goals towards fulfilling it.

4. Motivation

Motivation is a powerful force that shows how much you really want your intention or vision. Motivation is shown by how much time, effort and focus you are prepared to give it. If it doesn't work straight away, are you prepared to go back to it and change or fine-tune it? Would you continue to embark on changes, such as finding more resources or developing any skills required to give your intention the best possible chance of success? Perhaps when things don't work out, the universe or your own deeper self is asking how much you really want what you are pursuing. Remember, it's not simply about intention and visioning. In this process, you are also dealing with karma (thoughts, words and actions) or deep psychological imprinting. Are you prepared to make the consistent efforts required to re-imprint neutral matter into new creative forms, knowing that this can take time to become more tangible?

1. What is your level of motivation for the vision you have, on a scale of 0-10? ____

2. What do you think your level of motivation will be if it does not come into being in the time frame you had hoped? ____

If you wrote 8 or above, you are motivated. If it is lower than 8, you may need to go back to your life purpose, intention or vision to make sure that it is what you REALLY want. You may need to reconsider, or adjust it, until you find a vision that has a higher than 8 motivation. Or you may need to realise that you are a cruiser, rather than a navigator at this time. You can change this if you wish.

Motivation creates excitement and excitement creates motivation. Motivation and excitement may be called passion and it is highly contagious because it is able to formulate thoughts into being when they are sustained in a pure form. Many of us can be passionate for a short time. Personal development workshops thrive on being able to help people become passionate for a day or a week, but the passion often falls away when they settle back into everyday living. This is why it's important for us to develop the discipline to constantly revisit our intention and vision daily, so that we can remotivate ourselves and stay on track with what we are creating.

Some people who believe in the Law of Attraction theory say that you have to remain strongly focussed for at least three weeks to allow a manifestation to be formed. I prefer not to give a specific time frame, as I believe it can be shorter or longer than this, according to karmic or psychological imprint, as discussed at length in this book. Light karma can imprint very quickly, while mid-strength, mixed karma can take much longer and depend on the ability to be resilient and consistent. Fixed karma may not be imprinted in this life at all. Hence, we don't always get everything that we think we want.

As I have explained before, if all your unconscious drivers are in congruence with your conscious wishes, it is likely that neutral matter can be imprinted relatively easily. If all is in line (going in the same direction), then there is no reason why it should not come into being if you can maintain your focus on imprinting it. However, if you become aware of self-sabotaging thoughts or fears entering your mind, you may benefit from some professional help to resolve the psychological block of belief or emotional state involved.

By utilising a high motivation for your dream, you will need to spend a lot of your free time focussing on your vision and charging it up with the emotion of excitement and enjoyment, as if it's already here. This requires some perseverance and discipline to sustain the vision because it can take some time to form.

5. Courage

Courage is necessary on this journey; the courage to stand out and be noticed, and to present yourself to the world in the best way possible. Wealth creation requires several major shifts in consciousness, which includes a change from the mediocre to the great, or from cruiser to navigator. In addition to the mind shift, it requires courage to stand out from your peers and to mould your personal, family or cultural boundaries into something different, unique and successful. By embarking on this challenge, you will be testing and extending your view of yourself and stepping into a greater image, so your sense of worthiness is a vital component as to how great you allow yourself to be. By daring to be great, you are taking full responsibility for yourself and for what goes well or not in navigating and creating your life. This requires courage that we all have somewhere. We all learned how to walk and talk, read and write, and that took courage.

6. Action

Once you have your intention, worthiness, motivation, courage and vision clear, the next step is action. The universe will come forward to assist you, but you are the creator. This means that action with creative forces is an important factor. Your willingness to come out of your comfort zone to recreate yourself is necessary. The desire that created the intention and vision is yours, so you are likely to be required to be involved in its formation. Of course, you can test it out. You can simply envision and see if it comes into being within what you consider to be a reasonable time frame, in which case, you are dealing with light karma. If it doesn't form quickly and easily, you know that your fuller involvement and action is required to deal with heavier karma.

Action is important. Unless your vision is materialising by itself due to a strong destiny, it is your responsibility to get out of your comfort zone and act. Put your thoughts and beliefs into doing, as well as being. Do so in a manner that affirms what you are creating in a positive way. Of course, you can try it without action, if you like, and see what, if anything, happens for you. If it works out, that's great.

However, if the bills are piling up while you are creating your dream, don't give up. Take action. Perhaps find a job to support you as your dream is finding form. By doing nothing and allowing the energy of fear or deprivation to rise, this will do great harm to your creation, so being proactive and supporting you while the intention is solidifying, has to be a positive move. Much more harm can be done if you don't act in a practical way to alleviate disaster and allow the outpouring of the negative messages of fear, doubt, anxiety and stress to take form. Of course, at times it may be necessary to let go of pride or ego to change your strategy so that you can find a way to manifest in a more positive way.

We are physical beings in a material realm who need food and shelter, and are required to pay our way as adults and take full responsibility for ourselves and our families. While basic physical needs are paramount, there are also many things that are not essential to have if we are experiencing financial hardship. If we live beyond our means, it may be that we are being pushed to look at our beliefs and possibly sacrifice our pride or ego to let go of non-essential luxuries. These may all be signs that what we are doing is not in alignment with creative forces. Some fine-tuning or even major inner and external shifts may be necessary to put our finances in order, so that we can create abundantly.

I have come across many people who are in collapsing financial situations, but continue on as if nothing is wrong. They often have a view that if they were to start to worry about the real situation of losing their home, job, car, relationship etc., this would be showing a lack of faith in their magnetic attraction powers and ruin their ability to create their dream. They seem to have lost sight of the fact that it is already ruined by the fact that it's not working. They appear to have an inability to assess the reality of their situation to take action in a common-sense and grounded manner. Just as, if your house was on fire, there would be an urgent need to put all other considerations on hold as you do everything possible to save your house, as a first priority.

Another argument such people have when challenged to change their strategy in the face of disaster is that wealthy people are often risk takers and never stingy in their spending. In this way, luck keeps flowing back to them. There is a healthy flow of finance throughout their life.

It is indeed true that those who have their lives in balance do not worry about finance and this is borne out by the fact that what they are doing is working well and is sustainable. The fact that what they are doing is working positively for them means that it is fine. Their beliefs and intentions are in alignment with their actions.

However, for those where this is not working, their lives fall apart while they desperately hold onto a structure that is patently unsustainable. Something is out of alignment. This could be many things, such as the intention itself being out of tune with their purpose or there may be deeper causes, or they are in the midst of a karmic pattern that is calling them to make radical changes to their thoughts, actions or emotional state. So, don't be afraid to change your response according to the situations that you face.

Successful people may appear to take risks and get out of sticky situations, and perhaps they do. Much like a tightrope walker, they appear to wobble and keep their balance and somehow stay grounded enough, even while they soar high in the air. This amount of skill and intuition must be earned from deep experiences over time. Perhaps this is the real secret of their success.

In non-urgent situations, it is helpful to take action to give your creation a place to take seed. Prepare the ground and perhaps hone your skills and put yourself in the right locations to meet those who can help you on your way as you keep your focus and motivation sharp and alive.

When I was going through my communication problems mentioned earlier, it seemed to me that there was no other way out other than sorting through it, one issue at a time. I could have 'given up' and said 'it's too hard' or left it until a 'better time', but I may well have jeopardised my business in the process, which was my livelihood. I did have a choice. I could do nothing or I could sort it out with positive action.

When you take action, how you approach the situation is important. Intention is very powerful and, in this time of new ways of thinking, competition is a thing of the past. It is more about being the best you can be and realising who you are and offering something to the world that is of benefit. Knowing that only those who will benefit from what you offer will be attracted. Interestingly, there is no need for competition if we are being rich and spiritual because competition feeds the reality of winning and losing by competing for limited top positions or resources at the expense of others. On the other hand, cooperation is a joining with creative forces and with likeminded forces and people that support growth for all. Each person can shine in their own unique way because, even though we are all the same, no one is quite like you or me. So, find support or hang out with like-minded people if you can. Competition involves an attitude of winner and loser, whereas a cooperative attitude involves growth into areas that are often unoccupied, so that you don't have to put someone else out of business to do well. The need to compete is riding on the old notion of scarcity and having to fight for limited resources or places. Cooperation and creativity are well matched in being able to form unique ideas and projects. Such an attitude shows a generosity of spirit and a faith in abundance.

By looking at your own situation, you can ask yourself the following questions:

- Am I in a location that is conducive to what I am creating?
- Do I have the appropriate connections to help me with my dream?

If you find that these factors are not conducive to your success, then you may need to orientate yourself towards more conducive factors, first with your imagination and then by communication and action. There is a need to prepare the environment so that neutral matter has fertile ground in which to grow. Depending on the dream you have, you may need to acquire the appropriate resources or environment.

This is a tricky area because, on the one hand, you need to dream and have faith that natural creative forces will manifest into reality while, on the other, you do need to be actively involved in your mind with clear vision and intention, and also be actively organising the necessary resources and environment where you can. However, if you are too focussed on the practicalities and include a strong will or forcefulness in the process, this may in fact show too little faith. As I have mentioned before, there is a difference between will and intention and, if you use an aggressive, narrow will, your intention may not come into being. A delicate balance of common sense, creative projection and faith needs to be found.

Action and imagining that you already have what you are creating is part of the creative process so, being with others in that field or making the connections of those in the area where you are heading, is a very productive path to take. You are moving your consciousness into the field where you are creating something special.

For many, wealth creation involves being the best you can be, in terms of presentation, service, knowledge, skills or product. It may take several years to perfect your art or profession to be at the top of your game and have peak confidence in what you are doing or being, or offering to the world. So, enjoy the challenge and your journey. Alternatively, wealth creation can happen now if everything lines up with your action lines up with your action.

Skills and Knowledge

By looking at action, consider the knowledge and skills you need to create your vision. These are your resources. If you already have them, fine-tune them and make them as sharp or as potent as you can and, if you require more skills, you will need to consider how you are going to acquire them.

Most people need to be in an industry or area of work for several years before they can consider themselves expert or knowledgeable in that field, unless they have a strong destiny for fame and fortune.

To be the best that you can be, you need to be an expert.

Are you prepared to dedicate the time, effort and, possibly, practise required for you to be considered an expert in your field of knowledge or practice?

Make a plan of how you are going to gain the resources you think you need and make it part of your vision. See it a a challenge and not a struggle. View the end product of having received the resources you need while being open to opportunities opening up as avenues towards creating your reality. You may need to be ready to go outside your comfort zone to expand your knowledge, experience and learn new skills.

7. Gratitude

Finally, having faith in your vision and not allowing any negative thoughts to come into your awareness, is a key to becoming rich and spiritual.

A generosity of spirit is required in this new way of thinking. No one can steal your essence or your creation because only fear and doubt can do that. So, by feeling your worthiness and abundance, you can easily feel the ease of being generous with others. When dealing with others, being generous by never giving short measure, is important. Always give good value and a full measure of what you have agreed to, with a generous heart. If you give of yourself and your services generously, it must surely come back to you at some point and, hence, become a continued cycle of abundance. Being generous can only be of benefit to everyone. I am not suggesting that you let go of your own or others' personal boundaries here. Just be generous in a balanced and business like manner in business matters, and have a social or friendly manner in others. Don't give so much that you ensnare others with guilty feelings of having to pay you back in some way. Interactions are best done with an air of completion, fairness and justice on each side. In this way, each can feel free to connect with the other at another time due to former interactions having been so joyful and fruitful.

If you are not in the place, business or job that you would like to be in yet, act as if you are already there. Do your best at your present position and be open to new possibilities.

To ensure a positive imprint of your vision, the final requirements are gratitude and faith. Make sure that you are constantly noticing all of the gifts in your life. Simple things like your home, food, people, health and events can be brought into focus regularly and not dismissed because they are already present or familiar. You will already have many things in your life for which you can be grateful. When you feel genuine gratitude, your heart will open and an involuntary smile will form. Feeling such gratitude can only send out positive vibrations and ensure that pleasure and abundance continue to come into your life.

To feel genuine gratitude, you will need to accept your life, just as it is. Totally. Everything that has happened so far has brought you to this point and you are now reading this book on how you can make the most of your life. Those of you who've experienced tragedy or trauma may find it hard to let these go and may need professional help to do so. If this is the case, do it when you can. Take responsibility for yourself and find the best people possible to help you to free your mind and your emotions, so that you can heal and move towards acceptance and gratitude for all you have.

I talk about this and provide examples and references in my book, *Stardust on the Spiritual Path*. So, if you need help, find the best practitioners you can to help free your mind and your emotions so that you can live in acceptance and gratitude now.

To be in gratitude, you need to have an open and free mind and emotions so that you can choose to be in acceptance of everything so far in your experience. Be aware that this can be a lifetime of personal development for many people, but it is rewarding by bringing more peace and harmony into your life.

With acceptance and gratitude, you can find yourself frequently giving thanks for the simple things in life: a nice day, a pleasant conversation, a friend, sibling, partner, child or a nice meal. There are so many possibilities for each of you. Giving thanks each morning and night is very helpful to lift your mood and maintain a full heart and keeping good things flowing through your life. Language is important.

Don't say things like:

'I wish for...', as you may get stuck forever 'wishing'

Or

'I want...', as you may be forever 'wanting'.

Or

'I am trying to...', as you may be forever 'trying'.

Instead, give gratitude for what you are creating as if it's already there:

"Thank you for ..."

Remember that by giving thanks and being genuinely grateful for all that you already have, you are positively imprinting neutral matter. You are visioning and bringing up your positive feelings about your dream and charging your motivation.

It's up to you now to become Rich AND Spiritual.

Chapter 20

Enjoy the Journey

This brings me to faith. It is something that can't be taught and can only grow through experience and choice. There is only love or lack of love. Lack of love is simply a separation from love that shows itself in hate, sadness, anxiety, violence and so on, while love shows itself in such states as happiness, joy, peace, faith and trust.

You have already been creating your reality, though largely unconsciously, through tumultuous thoughts and feelings. Now, with this new knowledge, you can choose to take full responsibility for yourself and what is taking place in your mind (emotions) and change them appropriately. This may be through initially observing them and then gradually finetuning them, and progressively gaining control of your life and what you are creating.

Only once we have gone through the process of refining our beliefs and emotions to set them free can we realise the freedom and happiness that this brings and, with this, comes faith. Faith is a deep knowing and embracing of the love of everything, both around and within us. Faith is a knowing of the connection of the 'All That Is' in the universe, through love. Love is at the centre of everything and in symbiosis with creative form and neutral matter. It gives us the total freedom to create our own reality. If we have created pain, sadness and hurt and we can choose to transform these into joy and happiness.

You have always had this freedom, but you have not always been aware of it. Your soul journey has brought you to this point to seek a way for you to step into your greatness with an open, loving and resilient heart. Creating wealth is a vital part of your spiritual journey to rediscover your innate power to create the most glorious image of yourself by using the power of your mind and emotions in full cooperation with creative forces, as a celebration of prolific universal abundance. This is a spiritual and personal development journey where you have the task of coming out of the illusion that you are separate from universal love, to find that you are an integral part of it. You are in charge and in the driver's seat of how it develops and where it goes. You are and have always created what is in your mind, but now you know how to be in control of your mind, emotions and your creation. Thoughts create reality.

Now that you have this knowledge, you can use it to observe the contents of your mind. From this awareness, you can begin the process of fine-tuning your thoughts and creating your reality more consciously.

In terms of becoming rich and spiritual, putting these ideas into practice and training your mind to stay focussed will ensure your success. It can have no other result if you really believe that you are a creator and that you have the power to create your life. Once you are taking full responsibility for yourself, are accepting, grateful, resilient and practical, all that is left is faith. Faith is the final imprint on neutral matter. If you have faith, you are leaving no place for doubt or anxiety to muddy your vision. Of course, you must keep your feet firmly on the ground and, if something you hadn't thought of pops up as a vital element for your creation, then add it. This is your life. Make any changes required and thank universal energy for giving you this additional awareness.

Reread this book frequently to remind you of what and why you are making those inner changes. This book remains a motivation you can revisit at any time.

From a Vedic perspective, we honour creation by being the highest expression of ourselves that we can be. This may be through any of our senses, or intellectual, athletic or creative pursuits, so that to sing, dance, breathe or run, our hearts is in full agreement with 'All That Is,' can only enhance ourselves and the divine within us. Don't forget to live in love and grace, and enjoy the journey of being rich and spiritual.

RESOURCES

www.yildizsethi.com

www.familyconstellations.com.au   www.vedicastrology.net.au

www.rapidcorehealing.com

Special Offers

10% off Yildiz's certified online training

If you love the book then consider taking your practice further.

Simply scan the codes below to receive 10% off Yildiz's:

- Certified Family Constellations online training
- Vedic astrology online

Or go to: https://familyconstellations.com.au/buy-fc-training/

Family Constellations Online training with experiential learning- 12 weeks

10% discount coupon **BRFC10**

Or go to: https://vedicastrology.net.au/buy-your-va-course-now

Vedic astrology online 12 week training

10% discount coupon **BRVA10**

Family Constellations training is certified in Australia and allows the student to obtain insurance and immediately start earning income and helping others.

Please read on to learn more about Yildiz's online training courses.

Family Constellations Online training

Family Constellations is a modality that shows the underlying dynamics, entanglements and generational trauma of individuals in their family systems. Also how these manifest in the present in relationships, parenting, patterns, wellbeing and mental health and their ability to fulfil potential.

This may take place in groups and private sessions, in person or online. The process is brief, experiential, psychodynamic, solution-focused, phenomenological and client-centred. A powerful way to re-order our inner perception of who we are into healthier places. The Constellation process works at the core of who we are as human beings, in a way that is limited or inaccessible with other approaches: Particularly in such a brief intervention.

The process works at several levels of awareness and experience simultaneously. Intellectual, visual, somatic, emotional, energetically and generationally. For Relationships, family, parenting, relational bonding, generational patterns, generational (systemic) trauma and incest. This results in several levels of change taking place simultaneously, as multiple levels of neural pathways realign. Suitable for existing and new practitioners.

The training is fully online with experiential learning component.

Learn Vedic Astrology Online

Learn how to read the magic and mystery of Vedic astrology.

How Yildiz developed the course

After Yildiz was introduced to Vedic astrology she spent years in study, research and practice. She went to courses in India, USA and in Australia and took part in lots of personal study and hundreds of Vedic astrology books. She found some information really useful and applicable and lots of information, confused confusing and not helpful or accurate. She has put in hundreds of hours of study and practice to find out what works accurately.

This is what she offers you this this course.

An honest open and practical approach to Vedic astrology in looking at the soul's journey.

Learning Vedic Astrology

You will learn by listening. There is an audio for each lesson.

You will learn by reading. There are course notes and charts for each lesson.

You will learn by doing. There are exercises at the back of 11 lessons for you to test yourself.

You may check your answers with the answers section included.

You may repeat each lesson several times.

You will listen and work through the course notes at your own pace.

Do it as fast or as slow as you want – It's up to you.

The course is designed to build your knowledge as you go through it.

You will be shown how to develop your skills in practical applications as you are shown how to navigate through chart information and build up an analysis.

All that's left after this is, Practice, Practice, Practice and ENJOY

Stardust on the Spiritual Path, 2nd edition published in March, 2014. Amazon

Many are ready for the next step in consciousness in finding a belief system or form of spirituality to help them discover a higher meaning in life. Through exploring elements of mystical India with knowledge of modern psychological and personal development, we may create a new enriching perspective of our soul journey as stardust. Yildiz explores aspects of Karma, Vedic astrology, reincarnation, free will and destiny and the process of Family Constellations as a means of making the most of ourselves on our soul journey through relationships and self-discovery towards enlightenment through a character named 'Surya'. The author uses ancient and modern philosophies and Eastern and Western knowledge in looking through Surya's eyes. Each decision has consequences and Yildiz discusses those with a strong emphasis on the intricacies of relationship

Rapid Core Healing pathways to growth and emotional healing (2016)
Amazon

Rapid Core Healing Pathways for Growth and Emotional Healing presents a dual psychotherapeutic approach for working holistically in a new and innovative way with a wide range of mental health and wellness issues, rapidly. The author Yildiz Sethi comes from a science teaching background prior to her career as a psychotherapist and educator of counsellors, psychotherapists and coaches. Her work in this field has resulted in her creation of two new modalities of psychotherapy which she is pioneering to address the next step of growth in this area. Rapid Core Healing (RCH) is a dual modality consisting of Emotional Mind Integration (EMI) and Family Constellations (FC) that is designed to work with the personal conflicts that people face in life and systemic (family of origin) issues simultaneously.

www.ingramcontent.com/pod-product-compliance
Lightning Source LLC
Chambersburg PA
CBHW051945290426
44110CB00015B/2114